# COMPUTING MADE SIMPLE

The original and the best.

**ONLY £8.99** except where priced

**WORD 2000 MADE SIMPLE**

**PHOTOSHOP 5 MADE SIMPLE**

**WINDOWS 98 MADE SIMPLE**

MARTIN EVENING & P

P. K. McBRIDE

**THE INTERNET MADE SIMPLE SECOND EDITION**

FULL COLOUR EDITION

These books explain the basics of software packages and computer topics in a clear and simple manner, providing just enough information to get started. They are ideal for users who want an insight into software packages and computers without being overwhelmed by technical jargon

- ● **Easy to Follow**
- ● **Task Based**
- ● **Jargon Free**
- ● **Easy Steps**
- ● **Practical**
- ● **Excellent Value**

MADE SIMPLE BOOKS
An imprint of Butterworth-Heinemann
http://www.bh.com

forget to visit our website http://www.madesimple.co.uk

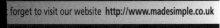

---

**NEW**
**AOL 4.0**
Keith Brindley
0 7506 4626 8 — 1999

**NEW**
**Access 2000**
Moira Stephen
0 7506 4182 7 — 1999

**NEW**
**Access 2000 in Business**
Moira Stephen — 1999
7506 4611 X — £11.99

**Access 97 for Windows**
Moira Stephen
0 7506 3800 1 — 1997

**Access for Windows 95 (V.7)**
Moira Stephen
0 7506 2818 9 — 1996

**Access for Windows 3.1 (V.2)**
Moira Stephen
0 7506 2309 8 — 1995

**NEW**
**Adobe Acrobat & PDF**
Graham Douglas
0 7506 4220 3 — 1999

**NEW**
**Compuserve 2000**
Keith Brindley
0 7506 4524 5 — 1999

**Compuserve (V.3)**
Keith Brindley
0 7506 3512 6 — 1998

**NEW**
**Designing Internet Home Pages** *Second Edition*
Lilian Hobbs
0 7506 4476 1 — 1999

**NEW**
**Excel 2000**
Stephen Morris
0 7506 4180 0 — 1999

**NEW**
**Excel 2000 in Business**
Stephen Morris — 1999
0 7506 4609 8 — £11.99

**Excel 97 for Windows**
Stephen Morris
0 7506 3802 8 — 1997

**Excel for Windows 95 (V.7)**
Stephen Morris
0 7506 2816 2 — 1996

**Excel for Windows 3.1 (V.5)**
Stephen Morris
0 7506 2070 6 — 1994

**NEW**
**Explorer 5.0**
P K McBride
0 7506 4627 6 — 1999

**Explorer 4.0**
Sam Kennington
0 7506 3796 X — 1998

**Explorer 3.0**
Sam Kennington
0 7506 3513 4 — 1997

---

**NEW**
**Internet In Colour** *2nd Edition*
P K McBride — 1999
0 7506 4576 8 — £14.99

**NEW**
**Internet for Windows 98**
P K McBride
0 7506 4563 6 — 1999

**Internet for Windows 95**
P K McBride
0 7506 3846 X — 1997

**NEW**
**FrontPage 2000**
Nat McBride
0 7506 4598 9 — 1999

**FrontPage 97**
Nat McBride
0 7506 3941 5 — 1998

**NEW**
**The iMac Made Simple**
Keith Brindley
0 7506 4608 X — 1999

**NEW**
**Microsoft Money 99**
Moira Stephen
0 7506 4305 6 — 1999

**NEW**
**Publisher 2000**
Moira Stephen
0 7506 4597 0 — 1999

**Publisher 97**
Moira Stephen
0 7506 3943 1 — 1998

**MS-DOS**
Ian Sinclair
0 7506 2069 2 — 1994

**Multimedia for Windows 95**
Simon Collin
0 7506 3397 2 — 1997

**Netscape Communicator 4.0**
Sam Kennington
0 7506 4040 5 — 1998

**Netscape Navigator (V.3)**
P K McBride
0 7506 3514 2 — 1997

**NEW**
**Office 2000**
P K McBride
0 7506 4179 7 — 1999

**Office 97**
P K McBride
0 7506 3798 6 — 1997

**NEW**
**Outlook 2000**
P K McBride
0 7506 4414 1 — 1999

**NEW**
**Pagemaker (V.6.5)**
Steve Heath
0 7506 4050 2 — 1999

**NEW**
**Photoshop 5**
Martin Evening
Rod Wynne-Powell
0 7506 4334 X — 1999

---

**NEW**
**Powerpoint 2000**
Moira Stephen
0 7506 4177 0 — 1999

**Powerpoint 97 for Windows**
Moira Stephen
0 7506 3799 4 — 1997

**Powerpoint for Windows 95 (V.7)**
Moira Stephen
0 7506 2817 0 — 1996

**NEW**
**Sage Accounts**
P K McBride
0 7506 4413 3 — 1999

**Searching the Internet**
P K McBride
0 7506 3794 3 — 1998

**Windows 98**
P K McBride
0 7506 4039 1 — 1998

**Windows 95**
P K McBride
0 7506 2306 3 — 1995

**Windows 3.1**
P K McBride
0 7506 2072 2 — 1994

**NEW**
**Windows CE**
Craig Peacock
0 7506 4335 8 — 1999

**Windows NT (V4.0)**
Lilian Hobbs
0 7506 3511 8 — 1997

**NEW**
**Word 2000**
Keith Brindley
0 7506 4181 9 — 1999

**NEW**
**Word 2000 in Business**
Keith Brindley — 1999
0 7506 4610 1 — £11.99

**Word 97 for Windows**
Keith Brindley
0 7506 3801 X — 1997

**Word for Windows 95 (V.7)**
Keith Brindley
0 7506 2815 4 — 1996

**Word for Windows 3.1 (V.6)**
Keith Brindley
0 7506 2071 4 — 1994

**Word Pro (4.0) for Windows 3.1**
Moira Stephen
0 7506 2626 7 — 1995

**Works for Windows 95 (V.4)**
P K McBride
0 7506 3396 4 — 1996

**Works for Windows 3.1 (V.3)**
P K McBride
0 7506 2065 X — 1994

*Includes New Titles for 1999*

# Excel 2000
# Made Simple
# Business Edition

## Stephen Morris

MADE SIMPLE
BOOKS

OXFORD AUCKLAND BOSTON JOHANNESBURG MELBOURNE NEW DELHI

Made Simple
An imprint of Butterworth-Heinemann
Linacre House, Jordan Hill, Oxford OX2 8DP
225 Wildwood Avenue, Woburn, MA01801-2041
A division of Reed Educational and Professional Publishing Ltd

℞ A member of the Reed Elsevier plc group

First published 2000

**British Library Cataloguing in Publication Data**
A catalogue record for this book is available from the British Library

ISBN 0 7506 4609 8

Typeset by Butford Technical Publishing
Icons designed by Sarah Ward © 1994

Printed and bound in Great Britain

FOR EVERY TITLE THAT WE PUBLISH, BUTTERWORTH-HEINEMANN
WILL PAY FOR BTCV TO PLANT AND CARE FOR A TREE.

# Contents

# Preface

Excel 2000 is the latest in a long line of spreadsheet applications, which has seen this grid-based software evolve from a simple number-crunching tool into a sophisticated data management and reporting environment.

Excel 2000 is part of the Office 2000 suite and, as such, is tightly integrated with the other programs in the package. As a consequence, reports and charts produced in Excel can be based on an Access database and transferred into a Word document or PowerPoint presentation in seconds.

As with all previous versions, the latest edition of Excel has a number of enhancements. Once again, the system requirements for running the software are considerably greater than for its predecessors. Office 2000 demands a minimum of a Pentium 75 MHz computer with 16 Mb of memory and 250 Mb of hard-disk space (much more if you intend to install the whole of Office 2000). If you want to run more than one application simultaneously – without which Office can be severely limited – you will need a minimum of an extra 4 Mb of memory for each application (in some cases, 8 Mb). Excel 2000 runs under Windows 95, Windows 98 or Windows NT.

This book provides business users of Excel 2000 with the information needed to get started with the program. No previous spreadsheet knowledge is required but it is assumed that the reader can perform the standard Windows tasks, such as clicking and dragging.

The fundamental aspects of Excel are covered in some detail and will give the reader a thorough grounding in the software and its operation. It should then be possible to build on this knowledge in order to make use of Excel's more sophisticated features.

This business edition of the book includes extra chapters on data management, pivot tables, external databases, presentations and Internet access. Using the information here, you will be able to link your Excel worksheets to Access databases, Word documents, PowerPoint presentations and many other Windows applications. You can also retrieve data from the Internet and publish your worksheets on the Web.

With a little practice, the most useful facilities are quickly mastered; Excel 2000 can then be applied to the processing of complex data sets and the production of professional-looking reports, presentations and Web pages.

## Examples on the Internet

You can find the examples from this book at the following Web site:

http://www.madesimple.co.uk

The site also includes substantial files of sample data, which you can download and use when experimenting with Excel's data management facilities.

## Acknowledgements

I would like to thank Microsoft Corporation for their assistance while this book was in preparation.

# 1 The main principles

# Introducing Excel 2000

The Excel spreadsheet program is designed to make the manipulation of information easy and fast. The program can process many types of data: from mainly numeric tables – such as balance sheets, sales returns and production schedules – to the sort of lists more usually associated with database programs. This book will show you how these various types of information can be handled.

To get Excel up and running, follow these steps:

1 Click on the Windows Start button, in the bottom left-hand corner of the screen.

2 Select the Programs option.

3 Select Microsoft Excel from the list.

The program is loaded and the Excel display will take up most of the screen.

Alternatively, if you created an Office 2000 folder on the desktop, double-click on the Excel icon.

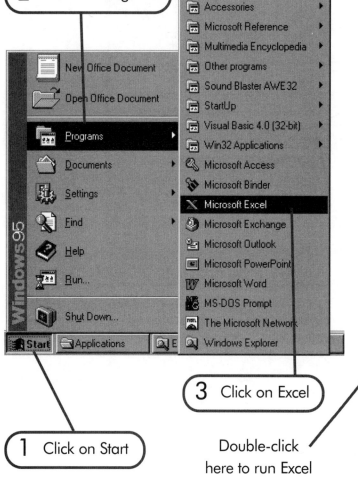

2 Move to Programs

3 Click on Excel

1 Click on Start

Double-click here to run Excel

In the Office Assistant:

☐ Type a query and then click on the Search button.

☐ Click on one of the suggested topics to display Help.

For more information on Excel Help, see page 8.

The first time you run Excel, the **Office Assistant** may be displayed (depending on how Office 2000 was installed). This animated picture can provide Help in a number of ways that may be attractive for new users, though existing users are likely to find it irritating.

You can type a query into the box and the Assistant will display topics that may be relevant.

Enter a query

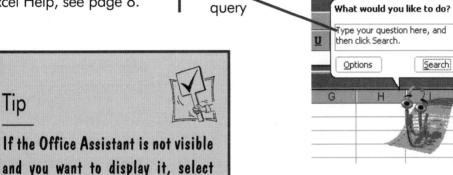

Click to search for Help topics

## Tip

If the Office Assistant is not visible and you want to display it, select 'Show the Office Assistant' from the Help menu.

To remove the Assistant from the screen, select 'Hide the Office Assistant' from the Help menu.

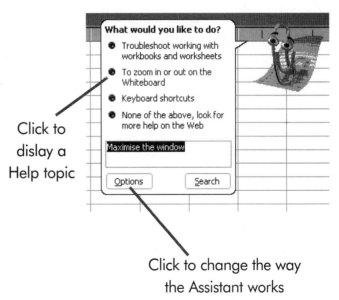

Click to dislay a Help topic

## Take note

The next time you start Excel, the Office Assistant will be as you left it.

Click to change the way the Assistant works

# Screen components

The guiding principle behind Windows is intended to be that it makes computer applications easier to use. Certainly the use of a mouse for selecting options is preferable to the complicated key-based commands that had to be memorised for older applications, and the use of icons and buttons with simple pictures on them can make the choice of actions easier. However, Excel 2000, in common with most modern Windows applications, provides a screen that is extremely cluttered and can be very daunting to the new user. The screen contains all the usual Windows features.

☐ The control menu leads to the standard Windows menu.

☐ The title bar is used to move the window (when not full size).

☐ The Minimize button converts the window to an icon.

☐ The Maximize button makes the window full size or reduces it to a smaller window.

☐ The Close button closes down the program.

☐ After clicking on the Maximize button to reduce the window size, dragging the corners and edges changes the window dimensions.

Close button: click to end program

Maximize button: window is initially full size

Title bar: drag to move window

Control menu: click for Windows menu

Minimize button: click to convert to icon

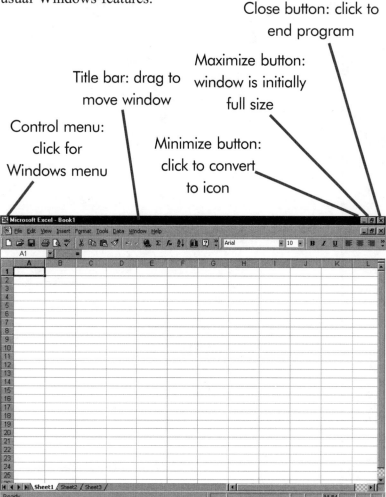

If the grid is in a separate, smaller window, click here

- The title bar tells you the title of the file.

- The menu bar has a set of drop-down menus giving access to Excel's features.

- The toolbar is a row of buttons and selection boxes which provide shortcuts to the menu options or quick ways of entering values.

- The sheet tabs and tab buttons let you move from one worksheet to another (see pages 94 and 97).

- The scroll bars allow fast movement within a sheet.

- The status bar is used by Excel for displaying messages and giving information, such as whether the [Num Lock] and [Caps Lock] keys are switched on.

- The main grid is where data is entered, and results displayed.

The main components of the display are listed briefly here, with fuller descriptions given later.

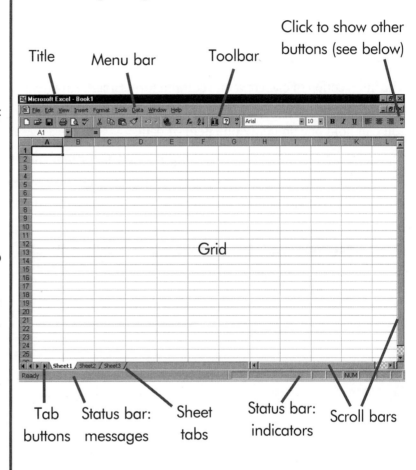

Title  Menu bar  Toolbar  Click to show other buttons (see below)

Grid

Tab buttons  Status bar: messages  Sheet tabs  Status bar: indicators  Scroll bars

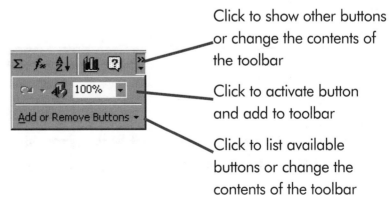

Click to show other buttons or change the contents of the toolbar

Click to activate button and add to toolbar

Click to list available buttons or change the contents of the toolbar

# The worksheet grid

In common with all other spreadsheet programs, Excel is organised around a simple grid system. The grid consists of a rectangular array of rows and columns and is called a **worksheet**. The columns are labelled with letters: A, B, C and so on; the rows are numbered from 1 down the sheet.

The intersection of each row and column forms a **cell**. Any item of data entered on the sheet is placed in one of these cells; each cell can hold one and only one item of data.

The cells are identified by combining the cell letter and row number. For example, the cell in the top left-hand corner of the sheet is A1. To the right of this is B1, then C1, and so on. The cells in the second row are labelled A2, B2, C2 etc.

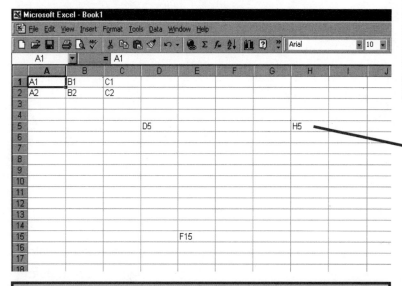

## Limits

Excel allows you to create very large worksheets.

☐ The first 26 columns are labelled A to Z, the next 26 are AA to AZ, then BA to BZ, and so on up to column IV (giving 256 columns in all).

☐ The rows are numbered from 1 to 65,536, giving over 16 million cells.

However, spreadsheets become unmanageable if they get too large.

Cell H5 is in column H, row 5

---

Take note

In practice, worksheet size is limited not by the number of cells available but by the amount of free computer memory.

---

Take note

An Excel file can contain several worksheets, which together form a workbook (see page 94).

## Options

☐ Click on the scroll bar arrows to move the display one row or column at a time.

☐ Click on the grey scroll areas to move by one screenful.

☐ Drag the buttons on the scroll bars to move by large amounts.

☐ Click on a cell to make it active.

☐ Press the keyboard's arrow keys to make an adjacent cell active.

☐ Press [F5] and enter a new cell reference to make any cell on the sheet active.

## Take note

**As you drag a scroll bar button, a pop-up label shows the row that will be at the top of the window or the column on the left when you release the button.**

# Moving around the sheet

The main difficulty with any spreadsheet program is that you can only ever see a small proportion of the worksheet at any one time. However, there are scroll bars to the right and below the grid, which allow you to move around the worksheet and see other areas of the sheet.

One cell is always **active**. This is the cell where data can be entered (initially A1). The active cell is identified by a thicker border. Any cell can be made the active cell by clicking on a cell, using the arrow keys to move around, or selecting a new cell with the menu options. Only one cell can be active at a time.

Reference of active cell                    Active cell

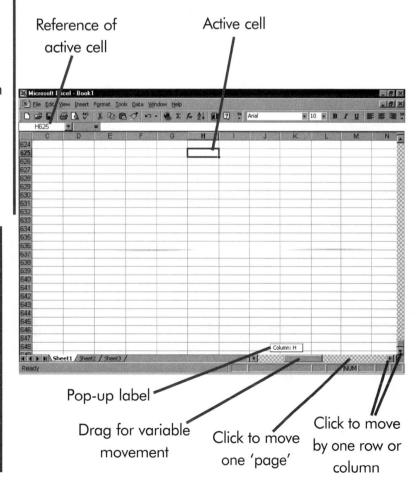

Pop-up label

Drag for variable movement

Click to move one 'page'

Click to move by one row or column

# Getting Help

Excel provides a dazzling range of on-screen Help options, offering step-by-step Help on every subject and a vast range of hints and tips. The best way to learn about Excel's Help facilities is by experience but the many options available can be a bit confusing at first.

If you want to use the more traditional style of Windows Help, turn off the Office Assistant by clicking on the Assistant's Options button and clearing the 'Use the Office Assistant' box.

The Help menu leads to either the Office Assistant or a full Windows Help program, and has links to the Internet and Help for Lotus 1-2-3 users. You can also re-install damaged or missing program files.

The Office Assistant lets you type in direct questions and then lists Help topics that matching your text. If you turn off the Assistant, the same task is performed by the Answer Wizard on the Help window. Alternatively, select a topic from the Contents list or find a topic by typing a word or phrase in the Index.

Labels are displayed under the toolbar buttons if you rest the pointer over them.

The status bar gives instructions when you select a menu option.

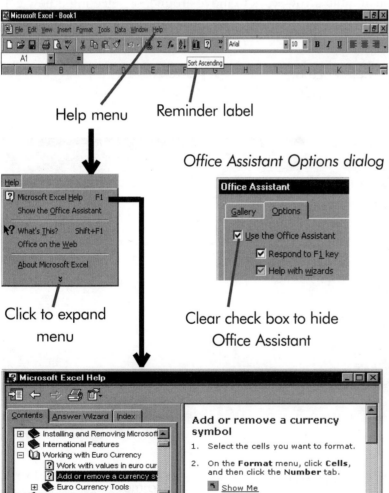

Help menu      Reminder label

Office Assistant Options dialog

Click to expand menu

Clear check box to hide Office Assistant

*Typical Help screen*

# Leaving Excel 2000

☐ Clicking on the Close button, choosing Close from the control menu or pressing [Alt]+[F4] ends the program.

☐ Selecting Exit from the File menu (or [Alt] [F] [X]) also closes Excel.

☐ Clicking on the Minimize button reduces Excel to an icon; the program and worksheet stay in memory.

☐ Clicking on another window pushes Excel to the back without closing it down.

☐ [Alt]+[Tab] and [Alt]+ [Esc] provide alternative methods of selecting other applications without closing Excel.

You can get out of Excel 2000 – either permanently or temporarily – using any of the usual Windows methods.

● If you close Excel down, then you will have to reload the worksheet at the start of your next session (or begin a new worksheet). Loading is described on page 25.

● If you temporarily move to some other Windows application, the current worksheet will be maintained in memory (but do save it first, just in case – see page 20).

Click here
...

... then here

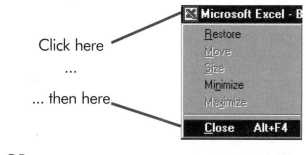

OR:

Click here
...

... then here

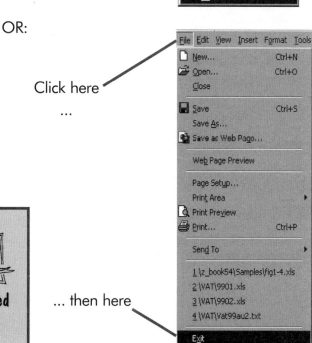

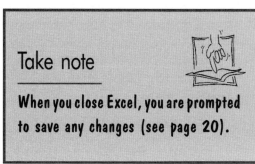

## Take note

When you close Excel, you are prompted to save any changes (see page 20).

# Summary

- ❑ Excel 2000 is loaded from within Windows in the same way as any other application.

- ❑ Data is entered onto a **worksheet**, which consists of a grid of individual **cells**.

- ❑ Columns are labelled with letters, from A to Z, AA to IV.

- ❑ Rows are numbered from 1 to 65,536.

- ❑ One cell is **active** at any time. A different cell can be made active by clicking on it; other areas of the worksheet can be viewed using the scroll bars.

- ❑ Help comes in the form of a Help menu, the Office Assistant, Help buttons, reminder labels and the status bar.

- ❑ The File menu, control menu and Close button provide all the usual Windows methods for leaving Excel 2000 (either temporarily or permanently).

# 2 Creating a worksheet

# Entering data

Excel always starts with a blank worksheet. Entering data is simply a matter of selecting a cell and then typing a value. You can enter numbers or text in any cell. As an example, create a worksheet with this simple table:

|   | A | B | C | D | E |
|---|---|---|---|---|---|
| 1 |   |   |   |   |   |
| 2 |   | TOTAL SALES: NORTH |   |   |   |
| 3 |   |   |   |   |   |
| 4 |   |   | 2000 | 1999 | % Change |
| 5 |   | 1st Qtr | 1092 | 1048 |   |
| 6 |   | 2nd Qtr | 718 | 623 |   |
| 7 |   | 3rd Qtr | 1953 | 1955 |   |
| 8 |   | 4th Qtr | 908 | 705 |   |
| 9 |   | TOTAL |   |   |   |

Don't worry about the appearance of the text to start with. It will look untidy when you enter it but you can tidy it up later by adding colour, changing column widths and so on.

Start by entering the labels around the main block of data:

1 Click on cell B2 so that it is the active cell.

2 Type TOTAL SALES: NORTH. As you do so, the text appears in the cell and, simultaneously, in the formula bar, above the column labels.

3 Press [Enter] when the text is complete. The cursor moves down to the next cell (in this case B3).

4 Now click on C4 to enter 2000, and D4 for 1999.

---

## Take note

**Excel recognises most of the entries as text and places them on the left of the cell. However, it treats 1999 and 2000 as numbers, putting them on the right of the cells. These values will be changed to text later (see page 14).**

## Tip

**You can also complete an entry by pressing one of the cursor keys or clicking on another cell.**

**5** Enter % Change in E4.

**6** Enter the row titles in cells B5 to B9. (Here, you do not need to click on the cells below B5 because the cursor moves down when you press [Enter].)

**7** Click on C5 and enter the value 1092.

**8** Fill in the other seven values in the cells from C6 to C8 and D5 to D8.

The totals will be calculated by Excel when a formula is entered (see page 28).

see page 28

---

**Tip**

If you start making an entry in the wrong cell, press [Esc] and no change will be made. Anything you have typed will disappear and the original cell contents (if any) will be restored.

---

Excel will always try to decide for itself what sort of data is being entered:

● If the value starts with a number, + or − sign, and contains only numeric characters, it is treated as a numeric value.

● If the entry begins with a + or − sign (and also contains letters) or an = sign, Excel assumes it is a formula.

● If the value starts with any other character, Excel assumes the entry is a piece of text.

Numeric values and the results of numeric formulae are always aligned on the right-hand side of the columns. By default, text entries are placed on the left.

Formula bar

# Text and number formats

If you want a numeric value to be treated as text, start by typing an apostrophe ('). This is a special code to indicate a text value and will not be displayed in the cell.

Excel assumes that a non-numeric entry is text, so there is no need to use the apostrophe except where there might otherwise be confusion:

● When the entry looks like a number

● When the entry starts with =, + or – but is not a formula

● When you want a real apostrophe to be displayed at the start of the label (start by typing **two** apostrophes).

To change the 2000 and 1999 labels to text:

1 Click on C4.

2 Type '2000 and press [Enter].

3 Click on D4.

4 Type '1999 and press [Enter].

The labels are now shown on the left of the cell.

## Take note

It is important to make the distinction between text and numeric entries, especially if you intend to use the contents of cells in a formula. Excel will not allow you to mix text and numbers in the same formula without using a special function. So if you want to add two numbers together, they must both be entered as numbers; and if you want to combine two pieces of text, both must be entered as text. For instance, to combine 'January' with '2000' to make 'January 2000', the value '2000' must have been entered as text, with an apostrophe in front.

## Tip

It is often easier to re-type an entry than to edit an existing entry. See page 16 for editing options.

## Tip

You can also centre a title in a row so that it stretches over several columns – see page 75.

# Numbers

For the General format, the type of display depends on the numeric value:

☐ Whole numbers (integers) are displayed with no decimal point (e.g. 123).

☐ Decimals are shown with as many decimal places as are needed, and with a zero to the left of the decimal point for numbers less than 1 (e.g. 12.3, 1.23, 0.123, 0.0123).

☐ Very large and very small numbers are given in Scientific format (e.g. 1.23E+09) – see page 62. This format is also sometimes called Exponential format.

☐ If the cell is too narrow to show a complete number, it is filled with # marks (though the number is still safely held in memory).

Numbers are displayed using the **General** format, unless you specify otherwise. With this format, Excel selects the most appropriate style in each individual case, using the least number of decimal places possible (and none at all for whole numbers).

In many cases this leads to an untidy display and you will want to change the format; details of how to do this are given in Chapter 7.

| | A | B | C | D | E | F | G |
|---|---|---|---|---|---|---|---|
| 1 | | | | | | | |
| 2 | | | | | | | |
| 3 | | | | | | | |
| 4 | | Integers | Decimals | Exponential | | Narrow | |
| 5 | | | | | | column | |
| 6 | | | | | | | |
| 7 | | 1 | 1.2 | 6E+19 | | ##### | |
| 8 | | 32 | 4.708 | 2.304E+11 | | ##### | |
| 9 | | 623 | 2.94571 | 3.462E+13 | | ##### | |
| 10 | | 1752 | 0.23 | 4E-10 | | ##### | |
| 11 | | 22385468 | 0.00004 | 6.23E-14 | | ##### | |
| 12 | | | | | | | |
| 13 | | | | | | | |
| 14 | | | | | | | |
| 15 | | | | | | | |

## Take note

You can apply different formats to individual cells or groups of cells. For instance, you can put a monetary symbol in front of money amounts or separate thousands with commas – see Chapter 7. You can also design your own format – see page 68.

# Simple editing

If you make a mistake, it's easily put right; there's no need to start all over again. The contents of any cell can be replaced or revised with very little effort.

Displayed value temporarily truncated during editing

Editing cursor

Formula bar

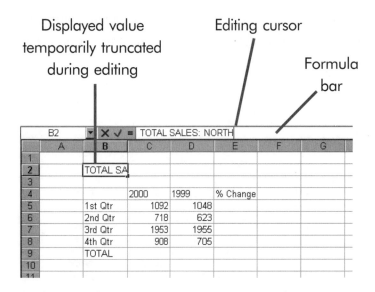

To edit the contents of a cell:

1 Click on the cell that contains the incorrect value. The value or formula appears in the formula bar.

2 To replace the value altogether, just type a new entry; there's no need to delete the existing value.

3 To change the value, click on the formula bar. Use the cursor keys or mouse to position the cursor within the value, then use the [Delete] key to erase the character to the right of the cursor or the [Backspace] key to delete to the left. New characters can be inserted at the cursor position.

You can also edit in the cell itself by double-clicking on the cell – the effect is the same.

## Tip

You can use the Windows cut-and-paste facilities to transfer text between applications. For example, [Ctrl]+[V] pastes text from the Clipboard into the current cell; [Ctrl]+[C] copies the contents of the current cell or highlighted text from the formula bar; [Ctrl]+[X] deletes the contents of a cell or highlighted text and places a copy in the Clipboard. Clipboard data can be inserted into any appropriate Windows application.

## Basic steps

To delete the contents of a cell:

1 Click on the cell.

2 Press the [Delete] key. (This is a shortcut for the Edit | Clear | All command.)

### Tip

**You can delete the contents of several cells by marking a range (see page 34) and then pressing [Delete].**

If you realise a mistake is being made as you are entering data, you can press **[Esc]** to abandon the entry. Whatever was in the cell beforehand is unaffected.

However, if a wrong entry has been made, or the contents of a cell are no longer needed, it can be deleted.

Mistakes can usually be cancelled, even after completing an entry, by pressing **[Ctrl]+[Z]**. This **Undo** action restores the original contents of the last cell changed and can be used after editing, replacing or deleting the contents of a cell. Each time you press **[Ctrl]+[Z]**, another action is cancelled.

You can undo several actions at once by clicking on the Undo list button on the toolbar. The list shows the most recent actions and any that you mark are cancelled.

Similarly, the **Redo** option repeats actions that have been cancelled by Undo. The Redo option is included in the Edit menu below Undo; alternatively, press **[Ctrl]+[Y]**.

### Take note

**There is another way that is often used to blank out a cell: click on the cell, press the space bar and press [Enter]. However, this can cause problems in formulae that refer to the cell. Excel replaces the contents of the cell with a piece of text consisting of a single space and any attempt to include this in a numeric formula results in an error. Therefore, this method of 'blanking out' cells should be avoided.**

Most recent actions to be undone

Undo last action

Undo list

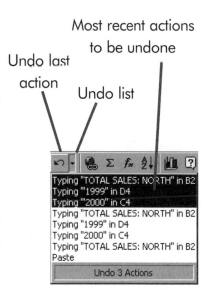

# Summary

- ❑ Data is typed directly into the cells.

- ❑ Excel decides whether each entry is text or numeric data; text is placed on the left of the cell, numbers on the right.

- ❑ Numbers and formulae can be treated as text by typing an apostrophe (') at the front of the text.

- ❑ Numeric values are displayed in the **General** format, with no more decimal places than are needed, and none at all for whole numbers (integers).

- ❑ To edit data, click on the cell, then retype or use the editing keys.

- ❑ To delete data, click on the cell, then press **[Delete]**.

- ❑ To cancel an action, press **[Ctrl]**+**[Z]**. Use the Undo button to cancel a series of actions and Redo to restore cancellations.

# 3 File operations

# Saving the worksheet

It is essential to get into the habit of saving your work regularly. The data you have entered so far exists only in the computer's memory and it will be lost unless you save it in a file before leaving Excel.

The worksheet data may also be lost if the program – or Windows – crashes (i.e. produces a fatal error message that results in the application being forcibly closed). This does not happen often but when it does, it's usually at the most inconvenient moment! So, save your work frequently.

Although you can undo most actions by pressing **[Ctrl] + [Z]**, there are occasions when you can damage a worksheet by some unintended formatting change or the application of an incorrect formula. Always save the sheet before any major change.

1 Click on File in the menu bar and then on Save in the menu that drops down. A standard Windows file box appears.

2 Double-click on the drive and then on the folder; do not store your files in the Excel 2000 program folder; use a new folder for your data. (The Save As window has a button for creating a new folder if necessary.)

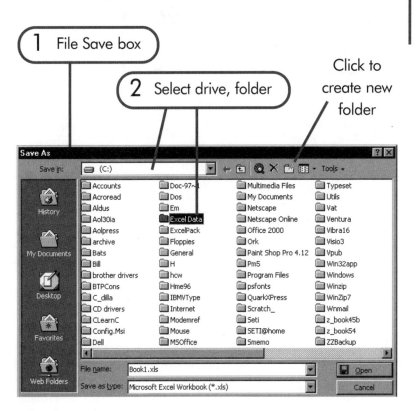

1 File Save box

2 Select drive, folder

Click to create new folder

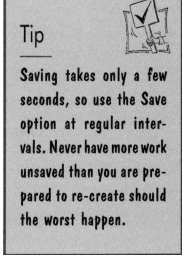

## Tip

Saving takes only a few seconds, so use the Save option at regular intervals. Never have more work unsaved than you are prepared to re-create should the worst happen.

**3** Type a filename, following the usual Windows rules. If the file may be used on DOS systems, restrict the name to a maximum of eight numbers and letters, with no spaces. Avoid using the other permitted characters, though the dash (-) or underscore (_) can sometimes be useful. Do not enter an extension; Excel automatically adds .XLS for you.

**4** Click on Save.

The file is saved, the new name appears on the title bar, and you can continue editing.

The next time you choose File|Save you will not have to supply a name; the current worksheet will replace the previous version in the file.

You will need to devise some logical naming scheme for your Excel files. Names need to be brief but remind you of what the files contain. Bear in mind that you may want to create several different versions of the same file, so allow for the inclusion of some further identification (e.g. Sales 2000 North Actual, Sales 2001 West Projected).

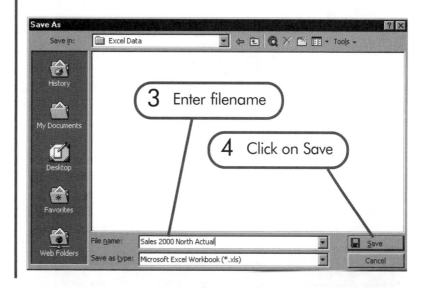

Toolbar shortcuts for File menu

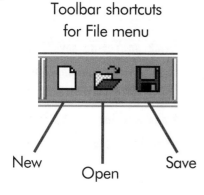

New    Open    Save

**Tip**

If you need to keep copies of previous versions of a file, do so by storing them in different folders. For instance, if you update files monthly, include the month and year in the folder name.

You can add other information relating to the file using the File|Properties option. Enter any relevant details and click on OK. Resave the file with File|Save.

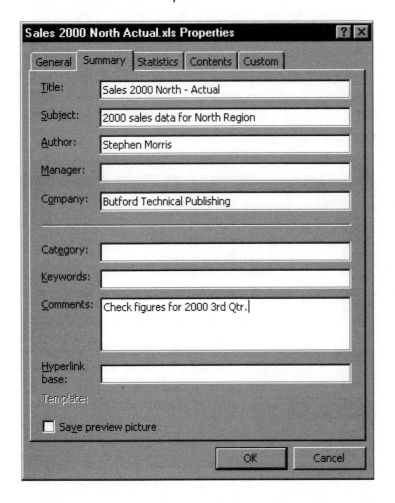

**Tip**

To resave quickly, just press [Ctrl]+[S] or click on the Save button on the toolbar.

If you want to save a new version of the worksheet, leaving the original intact, choose Save As from the File menu, instead of Save. You are then given the opportunity to enter a new name or choose a new folder. The original file will remain as it was when it was last saved. This gives you a simple way to use an existing file as the basis for a new one.

**Take note**

If you attempt to leave Excel without saving the changes you have made, the program will prompt you to do so. You are presented with three options.

Click on Yes to save the changes, No to abandon them or Cancel to continue working on the file without saving it.

# The worksheet window

## Tip

Unless it is essential that you see other windows while working on a sheet, keep the Excel 2000 window maximised. Otherwise, the screen can become very confusing.

The Excel 2000 display considered so far has actually consisted of two windows: the main Excel window and a subsidiary window containing the worksheet file. Initially, the subsidiary window is maximised, so it completely fills the parent window (the Excel window).

If you click on the lower of the two Maximize buttons, the second window will be reduced in size and the distinction between the two will become more apparent.

This is a useful option when you need to see two sheets at once (see page 98). At other times, you will have a greater workspace if you maximise the worksheet window.

Click here to reduce the Excel window size

Click here to reduce worksheet window size

Main Excel window (parent window)

Click here to maximise

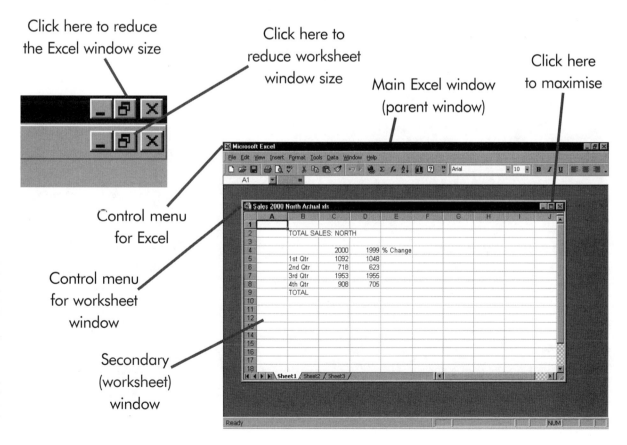

Control menu for Excel

Control menu for worksheet window

Secondary (worksheet) window

# Closing a file

You can close the secondary window without leaving Excel. This gives you a completely empty Excel window, into which you can load a new worksheet.

When the window has been closed, most options in the drop-down menus will be greyed out, indicating that they are unavailable.

There are several ways to close the worksheet file:

☐ Select Close from the File menu.

☐ Click on the secondary window's control menu and then on Close.

☐ Press [Ctrl]+[W].

☐ Click on the secondary window's Close button.

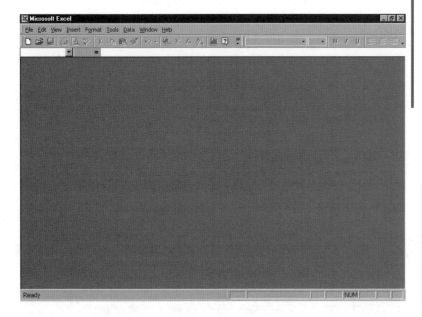

Tip

To start a new file, select File | New and then choose either the default Workbook or one of the supplied templates.

Alternatively, click on the New button on the toolbar. A blank worksheet is loaded (identical to the default Workbook).

Take note

You can save a worksheet as a template (with an **XLT** extension) rather than a normal **XLS** style. The template can be used as the basis for future worksheets.

# Loading a worksheet

There are three ways to load an Excel worksheet:

☐ Select Open from the File menu; choose the drive, folder and file from the file-list box.

☐ Click on the Open button on the toolbar as a shortcut to the File|Open option.

☐ Click on one of the most recently used files, listed at the bottom of the menu.

Providing you have saved your worksheet, it can be easily loaded again the next time you start up Excel 2000.

The File menu contains an option to load a worksheet (Open) and lists recently-used files. There is also a New option, which should be used if you want to start again from scratch.

There is no need to reload the worksheet if Excel has been temporarily suspended: just click on any visible part of the Excel window or, if it has been minimised, click on the Excel button at the bottom of the desktop. Alternatively, select Excel using **[Alt]+[Tab]** or **[Alt]+[Esc]**.

Start a new file

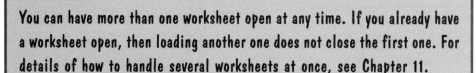
Re-open an existing file

## Take note

You can have more than one worksheet open at any time. If you already have a worksheet open, then loading another one does not close the first one. For details of how to handle several worksheets at once, see Chapter 11.

# Summary

- ❏ The File menu has options for saving and resaving worksheets. Files should be saved frequently (using the **[Ctrl]**+**[S]** shortcut keys).

- ❏ The Excel 2000 display consists of two windows: the main Excel window and a subsidiary window. Each has its own set of buttons for minimising, maximising etc.

- ❏ Closing the main window also closes the worksheet window.

- ❏ Close the worksheet window before starting a new sheet (unless you want two sheets open at the same time).

- ❏ To start a new worksheet, select File│New, then click on the default 'Workbook' icon or select a template from one of the tabs.

- ❏ To load an existing sheet, select File│Open or click on the worksheet name in the File menu.

- ❏ The toolbar has buttons for the New, Open and Save options.

# 4 Formulae

# Entering a formula

A **formula** is used to calculate the value of a cell from the contents of other cells. For instance, formulae may be used to calculate totals or averages, produce percentages or find the minimum and maximum values in ranges.

A formula consists of a mathematical or text **expression**, which refers to other cells or to constant values. The components of the formula are linked together by **operators** (+, – etc.) You can make forrmulae more readable by putting spaces on either side of the operators. Formulae must start with an =, + or – sign.

To enter a formula:

**1** Click on the cell where you want the result of the formula to be displayed (e.g. C9).

**2** Type the formula. For example:

   **=c5+c6+c7+c8**

(You can use either upper or lower case letters for cell references.) The formula appears simultaneously in the cell and the formula bar.

**3** Press [Enter]. The result of the calculation is shown in the cell.

When you click on this cell again, the formula is shown in the formula bar, where it can be edited. When you click on the formula bar or double-click on the cell, cell references in the formula are shown in different colours, and the cells concerned are highlighted by boxes in the same colours.

Current cell

Formula bar

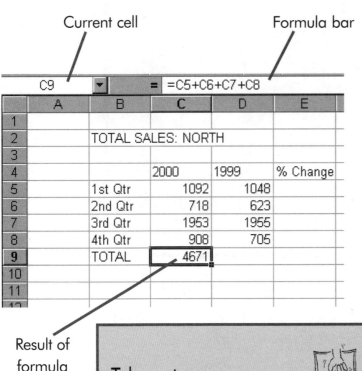

| | A | B | C | D | E |
|---|---|---|---|---|---|
| 1 | | | | | |
| 2 | | TOTAL SALES: NORTH | | | |
| 3 | | | | | |
| 4 | | | 2000 | 1999 | % Change |
| 5 | | 1st Qtr | 1092 | 1048 | |
| 6 | | 2nd Qtr | 718 | 623 | |
| 7 | | 3rd Qtr | 1953 | 1955 | |
| 8 | | 4th Qtr | 908 | 705 | |
| 9 | | TOTAL | 4671 | | |
| 10 | | | | | |
| 11 | | | | | |

C9 ▼ = =C5+C6+C7+C8

Result of formula

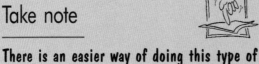

## Take note

**There is an easier way of doing this type of calculation, using the SUM function – see page 40.**

To edit a formula:

1 Click on the cell containing the formula.

2 Click on the formula in the formula bar.

3 With the usual cursor and editing keys, make the corrections.

4 Press [Enter]. The new result is displayed.

If you make a mistake that results in a formula which cannot be calculated (for instance, dividing by zero or referring to a text cell), Excel displays #VALUE! in the cell.

Other errors may be harder to identify and will not produce an error message. For instance, typing a – sign instead of + gives a valid answer but produces the wrong value.

Error in formula

| C9 | ▼ | = | =C5+C6+C7+B8 |
|----|---|---|--------------|

|  | A | B | C | D | E |
|---|---|---|---|---|---|
| 1 |  |  |  |  |  |
| 2 |  | TOTAL SALES: NORTH |  |  |  |
| 3 |  |  |  |  |  |
| 4 |  |  | 2000 | 1999 | % Change |
| 5 |  | 1st Qtr | 1092 | 1048 |  |
| 6 |  | 2nd Qtr | 718 | 623 |  |
| 7 |  | 3rd Qtr | 1953 | 1955 |  |
| 8 |  | 4th Qtr | 908 | 705 |  |
| 9 |  | TOTAL | #VALUE! |  |  |
| 10 |  |  |  |  |  |
| 11 |  |  |  |  |  |

Error indicator

# Calculation options

Excel recalculates the worksheet whenever you make a change to any item of data. The program adopts an intelligent approach; only those formulae that are affected by the change are recalculated, and the calculations are done in a logical order. The formulae that refer to the changed cell are recalculated first; if this results in changes to other cells, then any further formulae that are affected are also calculated, and so on.

This seems impressive when you first use a spreadsheet program but can become tedious, particularly for large, complicated worksheets, where a full recalculation may take some time. In such cases, you can use the Options item in the Tools menu to switch automatic calculation off. Click on the Calculation tab and a range of options is available; clicking on Manual means that in future you will have to press **[F9]** to force a recalculation.

The Calculation tab from the Tools | Options menu gives you these alternatives:

☐ Automatic recalculates affected cells in logical order – the default.

☐ Automatic Except Tables recalculates everything except data tables (see on-line help for more details).

☐ Manual recalculates the sheet only when you press [F9].

Leave Recalculate Before Save switched on – this forces a recalculation in Manual mode whenever you save the file.

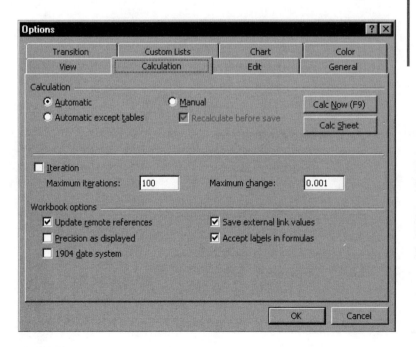

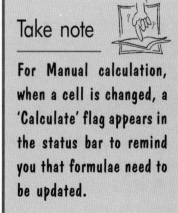

Take note

For Manual calculation, when a cell is changed, a 'Calculate' flag appears in the status bar to remind you that formulae need to be updated.

# Operators

The following numeric operators are recognised:

- ^    Raising to the power (e.g. $2\wedge3$ is $2^3$)
- *    Multiplication
- /    Division
- +    Addition
- –    Subtraction

You can also use:

- –    Negation (in front of a number)
- %    Percentage (after a number)

For text formulae:

- &    Combines strings (concatenation)

Five main arithmetic operators are used to determine how values are combined. A formula consists of an alternating sequence of values and operators, usually starting and ending with a value (the only exceptions are the use of a minus sign to negate a value and the percentage symbol).

The calculation is not carried out from left to right but according to the following rules:

- Raising to the power (^) is done first (also called **exponentiation**).

- Next come any multiplications and divisions (* /).

- Finally, additions and subtractions (+ –) are performed.

For text calculations, only the & operator is allowed. This adds one piece of text to the end of another. For example:

    = "Mon" & "day"

This formula produces the result 'Monday'. You cannot use + to combine text in a formula.

---

## Take note

Plus and minus signs are also used in numbers that are displayed or entered using the Scientific format – see page 62.

## Take note

You can precede a value with a minus sign (–) to negate it or follow a value with a percentage sign (%). For example, 2*–3 gives –6; multiplying by 5% is the same as multiplying by 0.05. Negations and percentages are done before any of the other operations.

# Using brackets

You can use brackets (parentheses) to change the order of calculation. Anything inside a pair of brackets is calculated first.

For example, the percentage change in E5 is calculated by:

### = (C5 – D5) / D5

The brackets are essential here; if there were no brackets the division would be carried out first, giving a result of 1091 (i.e. C5 – 1).

| E5 | ▼ | = | = (C5 - D5) / D5 | | |
|---|---|---|---|---|---|
| | A | B | C | D | E |
| 1 | | | | | |
| 2 | | TOTAL SALES: NORTH | | | |
| 3 | | | | | |
| 4 | | | 2000 | 1999 | % Change |
| 5 | | 1st Qtr | 1092 | 1048 | 0.041985 |
| 6 | | 2nd Qtr | 718 | 623 | |
| 7 | | 3rd Qtr | 1953 | 1955 | |
| 8 | | 4th Qtr | 907 | 705 | |
| 9 | | TOTAL | 4670 | | |
| 10 | | | | | |
| 11 | | | | | |
| 12 | | | | | |

Number of decimal places will be changed later

## Main points

☐ Calculations start inside the innermost pair of brackets and work outwards.

☐ Every opening bracket must have a corresponding closing bracket (Excel highlights the matching opening bracket for you every time you type a closing bracket).

☐ You can nest up to seven pairs of brackets (see opposite).

Tip

**Sometimes brackets are used for clarity, even when not strictly necessary. For example:**

**(C5 \* 3) + (D5 \* 5)**

**rather than:**

**C5\*3+D5\*5.**

Tip

**You can make formulae easier to understand by including spaces on either side of the operators. Excel ignores any spaces within a formula.**

You can also **nest** brackets: i.e. place one set of brackets inside another.

For example:

= ((100 − (A8 + 1) * 5) + 0.5) / 10

If the value of A8 is 7, the formula is calculated as follows:

((100 − (7 + 1) * 5) + 0.5) / 10

= ((100 − 8 * 5) + 0.5) / 10

= ((100 − 40) + 0.5) / 10

= (60 + 0.5) / 10

= 60.5 / 10

= 6.05

Don't let your formulae get too complicated. It is better to split a complex formula over several cells than to build them all into a single formula. This allows you to find errors more easily and to check intermediate values. For example:

In D5:       = A8 + 1

In D6:       = 100 − (D5 * 5)

In D7:       = (D6 + 0.5) / 10

# Ranges

Many operations within Excel require you to mark out **ranges** of cells. For example, you may want to add together all the numbers in a range of cells; you will also want to change the display format for ranges of cells (see Chapter 7).

A range is a group of cells that form a rectangle. The range is identified by the cells in the top left-hand and bottom right-hand corners of the rectangle, separated by a colon. For instance, the range reference A1:B3 identifies a range containing six cells: A1, A2, A3, B1, B2, B3.

A range can be anything from a single cell to the entire worksheet.

To mark a range on the worksheet:

1 Move the pointer to the cell in the top left-hand corner of the range.

2 Press and hold the mouse button, then drag the pointer to the cell at the bottom right-hand corner of the range.

3 Release the mouse button; the range is highlighted.

Alternatively, click on the first cell, press and hold [Shift], then click on the last cell.

|   | A | B | C | D | E | F | G |
|---|---|---|---|---|---|---|---|
| 1 |   |   |   |   |   |   |   |
| 2 |   |   |   |   |   |   |   |
| 3 |   | B3:B3 |   |   | D3:F3 |   |   |
| 4 |   |   |   |   |   |   |   |
| 5 |   |   |   |   |   |   |   |
| 6 |   | B5:B8 |   |   | D5:F8 |   |   |
| 7 |   |   |   |   |   |   |   |
| 8 |   |   |   |   |   |   |   |
| 9 |   |   |   |   |   |   |   |
| 10 |   |   |   |   |   |   |   |
| 11 |   |   |   |   |   |   |   |

Start dragging here

Finish dragging here

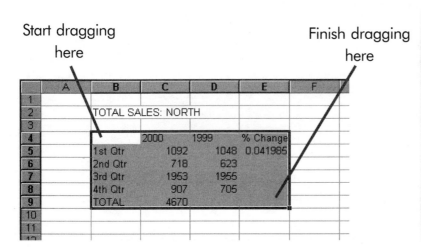

|   | A | B | C | D | E | F |
|---|---|---|---|---|---|---|
| 1 |   |   |   |   |   |   |
| 2 |   | TOTAL SALES: NORTH |   |   |   |   |
| 3 |   |   |   |   |   |   |
| 4 |   |   | 2000 | 1999 | % Change |   |
| 5 |   | 1st Qtr | 1092 | 1048 | 0.041985 |   |
| 6 |   | 2nd Qtr | 718 | 623 |   |   |
| 7 |   | 3rd Qtr | 1953 | 1955 |   |   |
| 8 |   | 4th Qtr | 907 | 705 |   |   |
| 9 |   | TOTAL | 4670 |   |   |   |
| 10 |   |   |   |   |   |   |
| 11 |   |   |   |   |   |   |

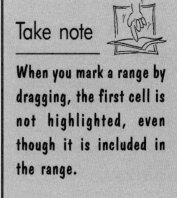

Take note

When you mark a range by dragging, the first cell is not highlighted, even though it is included in the range.

# Options

- ☐ To mark a single cell just click on it.

- ☐ To mark a whole row or column, click on the row number or column letter.

- ☐ To mark the entire worksheet, click on the square in the top left-hand corner of the worksheet.

You can highlight whole rows or columns, or the entire sheet by clicking on the worksheet borders.

You can select more than one range at a time by holding down the **[Ctrl]** key while you mark the blocks, rows or columns.

If you click anywhere else after you have marked a block, the block marking disappears.

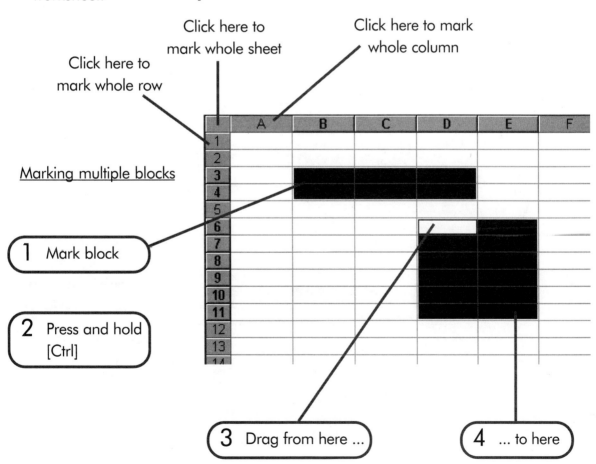

Click here to mark whole row

Click here to mark whole sheet

Click here to mark whole column

Marking multiple blocks

1 Mark block

2 Press and hold [Ctrl]

3 Drag from here ...

4 ... to here

# Names

Working with ranges can be cumbersome, particularly on large worksheets where a formula may refer to a range that is some distance away. So Excel allows you to attach a name to any cell or range. This name can be used in any formula in place of the cell or range reference.

Names can be up to 255 characters (far more than you should ever use), consisting of letters, numbers, full stops and under-score characters. Other characters are not allowed. The name should start with a letter.

Upper and lower case letters are treated the same but the name is stored exactly as you type it, so it is a good idea to mix lower case letters and capitals. When a name is referenced in a formula, Excel converts it to the same mixture of upper and lower case.

Basic steps

To add a name:

1 Mark the cell or range to which the name is to be applied.

2 Select the Name option from the Insert menu.

3 Click on Define in the sub-menu.

4 Type the name and press [Enter].

The names you create can be listed in the box above the column letters (where the cell reference is usually shown). Click on the arrow on the right of the box to see the list drop down.

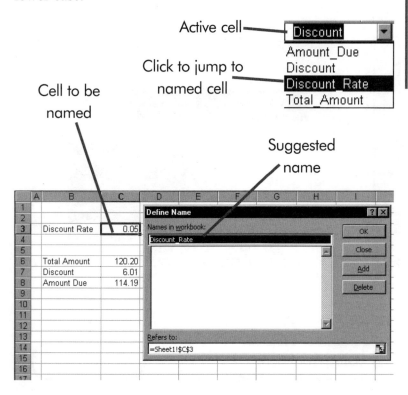

Active cell

Click to jump to named cell

Cell to be named

Suggested name

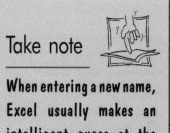

Take note

When entering a new name, Excel usually makes an intelligent guess at the name for you (for instance, it may select an adjacent label, replacing any spaces with underscores).

36

To use existing labels as names:

**1** Mark a range consisting of the labels and the cells to which they are to be attached.

**2** Select Insert | Name | Create.

**3** Identify the location of the names. For example, Left Column means that the names are in a column to the left of the data range.

**4** Press [Enter].

Active cell

| Total Amount | 120.20 |
| Discount | 6.01 |
| Amount Due | 114.19 |

**Create Names**   ? ☒

Create names in
☐ Top row
☑ Left column
☐ Bottom row
☐ Right column

[ OK ]   [ Cancel ]

To use a name in a formula, simply substitute the name for the cell reference. In the example in the illustration, the formulae for Discount and Amount Due were originally:

**= C6 * C3**

**= C6 – C7**

These can be changed to:

**= Total_Amount * Discount_Rate**

**= Total_Amount – Discount**

Names can either be typed in full or inserted by clicking on the required data cells as you are entering the formula.

Click for list of names            Formula using named cells

| Amount_Due ▼ | | = | = Total_Amount - Discount |

| | A | B | C | D | E |
|---|---|---|---|---|---|
| 1 | | | | | |
| 2 | | | | | |
| 3 | | Discount Rate | 0.05 | | |
| 4 | | | | | |
| 5 | | | | | |
| 6 | | Total Amount | 120.20 | | |
| 7 | | Discount | 6.01 | | |
| 8 | | Amount Due | 114.19 | | |
| 9 | | | | | |

## Tip

**Names are particularly useful where a range is referenced more than once on the worksheet. If you change the definition of the name so that it refers to another range, you will not have to change any of the formulae that use that name.**

**37**

# Summary

❑ Formulae are used for calculating cell values from the contents of other cells.

❑ Formulae start with an =, + or – sign, which is followed by an **expression**.

❑ Formulae are usually updated automatically every time a change is made to the data; alternatively, you can select Manual calculation mode, when calculations are only done if you press **[F9]** or the sheet is saved.

❑ Raising to the power (^) is always done first, followed by multiplication (*) and division (/), and finally addition (+) and subtraction (-).

❑ Values can be negated by putting a minus sign in front of them, or converted to percentages.

❑ Text entries can be combined with the & operator.

❑ Brackets change the order of calculation; the innermost expression is calculated first.

❑ Some operations require a **range** of cells. A range is a rectangular block defined by the top-left and bottom-right cells, separated by a colon (e.g. A1:B8).

❑ Names can be defined for cells and ranges, and these may be used in formulae.

# 5 Functions

# The SUM function

Excel contains a large number of built-in **functions**. These are special routines that can be used within a formula to perform particular tasks. For example, the most commonly used function is SUM, which calculates the total of all the cells in a specified range. Other arithmetic functions include AVERAGE to calculate the average of a range; MIN and MAX to find the smallest and largest numbers in a range; plus many others.

The function name is followed by a pair of brackets containing one or more **arguments**. If there is more than one argument, these are separated by commas. In the case of SUM, there need be only one argument: the range to be totalled. You can use either upper or lower case letters for the function and any cell references in the argument.

Functions are used in a formula in the same way as a constant value or cell reference. When the formula is calculated, the function returns a value which replaces it in the formula.

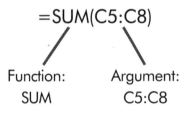

$$=SUM(C5:C8)$$

| Function: | Argument: |
|-----------|-----------|
| SUM | C5:C8 |

## Using SUM

The SUM function can be used in the Sales 2000 worksheet to replace the rather clumsy formula in C9.

1 Click on C9.

2 Start typing to replace the existing entry:

   **=sum(**

3 Drag the mouse pointer over the range C5:C8. As you do so the range appears in the formula.

4 Type the closing bracket and press [Enter].

## Take note

The SUM function can take more than one argument. For example, SUM(B6,C9:D12) returns the total of the number in cell B6 plus all the numbers in the range C9:C12.

## Tip

Although you can type the range directly into the function, marking it by dragging gives you a better chance of getting it right.

To use the AutoSum button:

1 Click on the cell where the total is required.

2 Click on the AutoSum button. Excel suggests the range to be totalled and marks it with a flashing outline. Check the range very carefully.

3 If the wrong range has been suggested, select a new one by dragging the pointer over it.

4 Press [Enter].

The SUM function has its own **AutoSum** button on the toolbar. This button lets you apply a SUM function with as few as three keypresses and button clicks. However, it requires some care; it is just as easy to get the sum wrong!

| NOW | ▼ | X ✓ = | =SUM(C5:C8) | | |
|---|---|---|---|---|---|
| | A | B | C | D | E |
| 1 | | | | | |
| 2 | | TOTAL SALES: NORTH | | | |
| 3 | | | | | |
| 4 | | | 2000 | 1999 | % Change |
| 5 | | 1st Qtr | 1092 | 1048 | 0.041985 |
| 6 | | 2nd Qtr | 718 | 623 | |
| 7 | | 3rd Qtr | 1953 | 1955 | |
| 8 | | 4th Qtr | 907 | 705 | |
| 9 | | TOTAL | =SUM(C5:C8) | | |
| 10 | | | | | |
| 11 | | | | | |

## Take note

AutoSum suggests the column of numbers above the current cell or the row to the left. If there are numbers both above and to the left, the block above is chosen. Any blank cells immediately above or to the left of the current cell are included in the block but if there are gaps in the numbers above or to the left, only those up to the gap are marked.

AutoSum

# Other functions

Excel comes equipped with a huge variety of built-in functions – over 200 in all. These fall into a number of categories:

- The **maths & trigonometry** functions include SUM and some more exotic variations (e.g. SUMSQ to calculate the sum of the squares of the values). All the most commonly-used trigonometric functions are available (such as sine, cosine, tangent), including functions to convert between radians and degrees.

- The **statistical** functions range from the simple AVERAGE function to a function for the chi-squared distribution (CHIDIST).

- The **financial** functions perform a comprehensive set of accountancy tasks. For example, DDB uses the double-declining balance method for calculating depreciation; NPV calculates the net present value of an amount that has been invested.

To use any function:

1 Type the formula up to the point where the function is required.

2 Type the function name and an opening bracket.

3 Mark the first argument (a cell or range).

4 If there is a second argument, type a comma (,).

5 Type further arguments and commas as needed.

6 Following the last argument, type a closing bracket and press [Enter].

## Help for functions

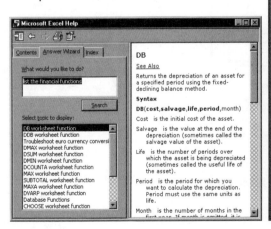

## Tip

There is a list of functions in the Formula Palette window (see page 44) but if you want detailed information on what is available you will have to look at the on-line Help. Each function appears in the Help Index. You can also get a list of the functions in a particular category by entering 'list the *category* functions' in the Answer Wizard.

● The **date & time** functions perform tasks such as extracting the month from a cell containing a date (MONTH) or returning the current date and time (NOW).

● The **text** functions let you work with text entries in cells; for example, LEN returns the length of an item of text, LEFT returns a string of characters from the left-hand side of the text and FIND scans a cell for a particular character or string. Any text included as arguments must be enclosed in double quotes (").

● The **lookup & reference** functions are applied to lists and tables; the **database** functions perform limited operations on database records.

● The **logical** functions apply logical AND, OR and NOT operations, returning results of TRUE or FALSE. Most importantly, they include the IF function for conditional calculations (see page 46).

● The **information** functions relate to Excel itself. For instance, CELL returns information about a specified cell, ISERROR tells you whether or not a cell contains an error (e.g. #VALUE!).

|  | A | B | C | D |
|---|---|---|---|---|
| 1 |  |  |  |  |
| 2 |  |  |  |  |
| 3 |  | Text Functions |  |  |
| 4 |  |  |  |  |
| 5 |  | LEN(b3) | 14 |  |
| 6 |  | LEFT(b3, 4) | Text |  |
| 7 |  | RIGHT(b3, 9) | Functions |  |
| 8 |  | MID(b3, 11, 3) | ion |  |
| 9 |  | FIND("Fun", b3) | 6 |  |
| 10 |  |  |  |  |

# The Formula Palette

There are many different functions in Excel and by far the easiest way of using them is through the Formula Palette. This provides a dialog box in which the functions are listed. When you click on a function, its purpose is shown at the bottom of the box.

The Formula Palette also provides a dialog box for entering the value for each argument, so you can be certain that you are supplying the correct number of arguments and that they are in the right order.

Each entry can be a constant value, or an expression. You can even **nest** another function by clicking on the small Formula Palette buttons (marked**fx**). Functions can be nested up to seven levels.

To use the Formula Palette:

1 Type the formula up to the point where you need a function.

2 On the toolbar, click on the Formula Palette button, marked with *fx*.

3 Select the Function Category to reduce the list size and click on the required Function Name. (Click on the All category if you don't know which set the required function is in.)

Select category ...

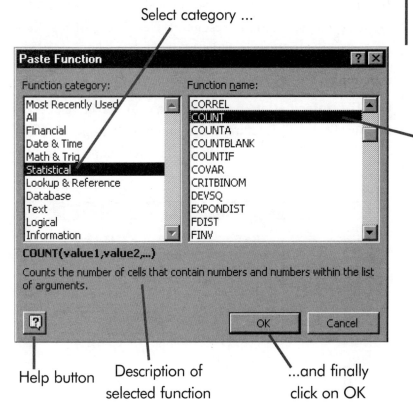

...then select function ...

COUNT(value1,value2,...)

Counts the number of cells that contain numbers and numbers within the list of arguments.

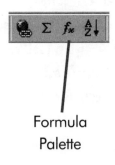

Formula Palette

Help button   Description of selected function   ...and finally click on OK

**4** Click OK to bring up the main palette, where the arguments can be entered.

**5** Click on OK and the function will be added to the formula.

**6** Click on the formula bar to add more elements.

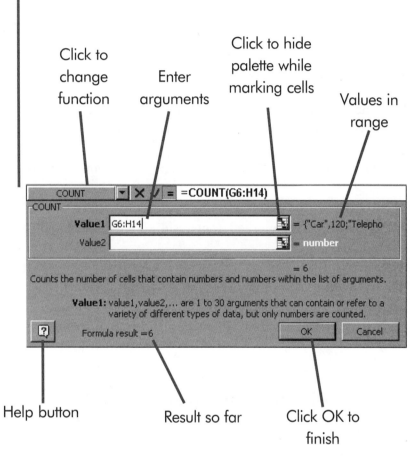

Click to change function

Enter arguments

Click to hide palette while marking cells

Values in range

Help button

Result so far

Click OK to finish

General error message for formulae

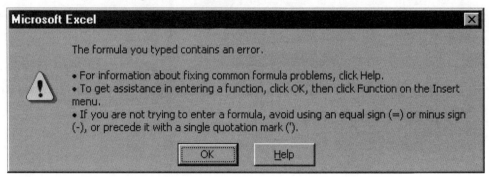

# The IF function

One of the most useful of Excel's many functions is the IF function. This **conditional function** compares two values and returns one of two results, depending on the outcome of the comparison.

The function has three arguments:

- The comparison to be performed (e.g. **C5<90** checks the value of cell C5 to see if it is less than 90)

- The value to be returned if the result of the comparison is true

- The value to be returned if the result of the comparison is false

The two return values may be constant values, text or further expressions.

## Operators

The following operators can be used in a comparison:

- <   Less than
- <=   Less than or equal
- >   Greater than
- >=   Greater than or equal
- =   Equal
- <>   Not equal

The IF function is included in the Logical category.

Current
values

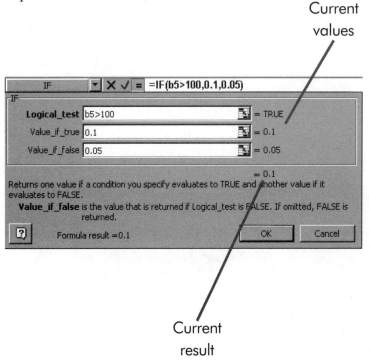

Current
result

## Tip

Don't make IF statements too complex; it is better to use a series of related functions where the result in one cell is passed to the next function in another cell. Otherwise, finding errors becomes very difficult.

Comparison expressions can be combined with the following logical operators:

AND True if both expressions are true

OR True if either or both expressions are true

You can also use the NOT operator, which reverses the result.

Formula in E5:
IF(B5>100, 0.1, 0.05)

For example, in the first illustration below, the Discount % column has a value of 0.10 if the Quantity is greater than 100, or 0.05 otherwise. The formula in E5 is:

**=IF(B5>100, 0.1, 0.05)**

This formula is copied over the range E6:E8. (See Chapter 6 for instructions on how to copy a formula.)

Complex decisions can be made by **nesting** IF functions. For instance, the discount calculation in the second illustration contains the formula in E8:

**=IF(Discount_Rate=0,0,IF(Discount_Rate=1,0.1,0.05))**

If the cell named **Discount_Rate** has a value of 0, the value returned is 0; otherwise, a further test is carried out, with a rate of 1 returning 0.1 and anything else giving 0.05.

You can also use the IF function to return warning messages if an input value is outside a permitted range.

| | A | B | C | D | E | F | G |
|---|---|---|---|---|---|---|---|
| 1 | | | | | | | |
| 2 | | | | | | | |
| 3 | | Quantity | Unit Price | Sub-total | Discount % | Discount | Total |
| 4 | | | | | | | |
| 5 | | 120 | 2.32 | 278.40 | 0.10 | 27.84 | 250.56 |
| 6 | | 86 | 3.45 | 296.70 | 0.05 | 14.84 | 281.87 |
| 7 | | 100 | 1.28 | 128.00 | 0.05 | 6.40 | 121.60 |
| 8 | | 200 | 0.95 | 190.00 | 0.10 | 19.00 | 171.00 |
| 9 | | | | | | | |
| 10 | | | | | | | |

Formula in E8:
IF(Discount_Rate=0, 0, IF(Discount_Rate=1, 0.1, 0.05))

| | A | B | C | D | E | F | G |
|---|---|---|---|---|---|---|---|
| 1 | | | | | | | |
| 2 | | | | | | | |
| 3 | | | | Discount Rate | 1 | (Enter 0, 1 or 2) | |
| 4 | | | | | | | |
| 5 | | | | | | | |
| 6 | | Quantity | Unit Price | Sub-total | Discount % | Discount | Total |
| 7 | | | | | | | |
| 8 | | 120 | 2.32 | 278.40 | 0.10 | 27.84 | 250.56 |
| 9 | | 86 | 3.45 | 296.70 | 0.10 | 29.67 | 267.03 |
| 10 | | 100 | 1.28 | 128.00 | 0.10 | 12.80 | 115.20 |
| 11 | | 200 | 0.95 | 190.00 | 0.10 | 19.00 | 171.00 |
| 12 | | | | | | | |
| 13 | | | | | | | |

# Summary

- ❑ A **function** is a built-in routine for performing some special action. For instance, SUM totals the values in a range.

- ❑ Functions consist of a keyword and a pair of brackets. The brackets contain one or more **arguments**, separated by commas. Some special functions have no arguments (e.g. NOW to return the current date and time).

- ❑ A **SUM** formula can be inserted using the AutoSum button on the toolbar.

- ❑ There are over 200 functions, in nine main categories. There are also 40 engineering functions, which may be added by running Office 2000 Setup.

- ❑ The **Formula Palette** provides an easy way to add a function to a formula, allowing you to choose the function and then fill in the arguments.

- ❑ The **IF** function returns two alternative values, depending on whether the result of some logical test is true or false.

# 6 Formula operations

# Copying formulae

In most worksheets, you will need to repeat the same formula in a number of cells or fill a range of cells with a similar formula. Excel makes it very easy for you to copy a formula to other cells.

In the example, the formula in C9 is=**SUM(C5:C8)** and this can be copied to D9. Excel does not make an exact duplicate of the formula; it assumes that the copied formula will refer to cells in the same relative position. That is, it sees the formula in C9 as an instruction to add together the contents of the four cells above. When the formula is copied, the effect is the same; the new formula adds together the cells above, becoming **SUM(D5:D8)**.

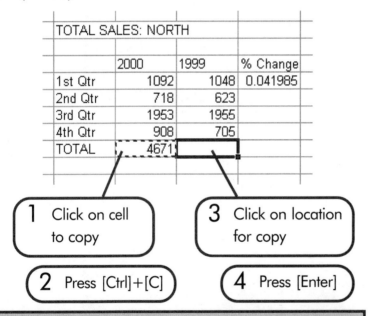

## Basic steps

To copy a single formula:

1 Click on the cell to be copied, so that it is highlighted.

2 Press [Ctrl]+[C] to copy the formula to the Windows Clipboard (or select Edit | Copy).

3 Click on the cell where the copy is to appear, or drag the pointer to highlight a range of cells.

4 Press [Enter] (or select Edit | Paste). The formula will be repeated in each of the highlighted cells.

## Take note

Anything already in the range to which you are copying will be replaced by the copied formulae or values.

## Take note

The same process can be used for cells that contain constant values or text strings; the values will be repeated in all the marked cells.

To copy a range of cells:

1 Mark the range to be copied.

2 Press [Ctrl]+[C] to copy all the formulae to the Clipboard.

3 Click on the cell that will be in the top left-hand corner when the range is copied. (You can also mark a range that will take multiple copies of the original range, providing it is exactly the right size and shape.)

4 Press [Enter] to complete the copy.

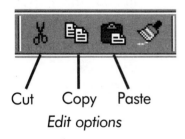

Cut     Copy     Paste
*Edit options*

Shortcuts
Cut     [Ctrl] + [X]
Copy    [Ctrl] + [C]
Paste   [Ctrl] + [V]

The % Change formula in E5 can be copied down the column by clicking on E5, pressing **[Ctrl]+[C]**, dragging over the range E6:E9 and pressing **[Enter]**.

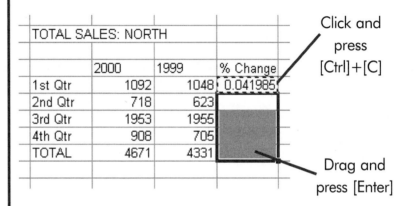

Click and press [Ctrl]+[C]

Drag and press [Enter]

When you copy further items to the Clipboard, the Clipboard toolbar is displayed. This contains an icon for each item you have copied; you can paste any of these items by clicking on the appropriate icon.

Paste object from MS Paint

Paste most recently copied item

Paste previous Excel item

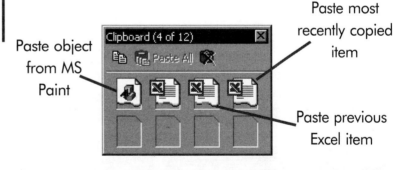

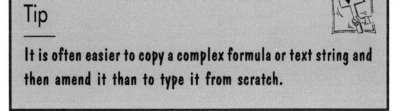

Tip

It is often easier to copy a complex formula or text string and then amend it than to type it from scratch.

# Relative and absolute references

When you copy a formula to another cell, any cell references are automatically updated so that they refer to the cell in the same relative position; these are called **relative cell references**.

Often, you want the formula to refer to the **same** cell, regardless of where the formula is copied. For instance, an invoice may take the discount rate from a single cell. To do this, each part of the cell reference is preceded by a $ sign; for example, a formula that refers to $C$24 will always use the value in C24, no matter where it is copied to. This is an **absolute cell reference**.

Sometimes you need to keep one part of the reference absolute while allowing the other part to change. For instance, the items in a table may be based on the values at the top of each column or on the left of each row. In these cases, the $ sign is placed in front of the part that is to remain unchanged. These are **mixed cell references**.

Formula in C6 uses three types of reference

| C6 | ▼ | = | = $B6 * (1-C$5) * (1+$F$2) | | |
|---|---|---|---|---|---|
| | A | B | C | D | E | F |
| 1 | | | | | | |
| 2 | **Gross Price Table** | | | | VAT Rate: | 17.50% |
| 3 | | | | | | |
| 4 | | | | Discount | | |
| 5 | | | 0% | 5% | 10% | 20% |
| 6 | | 1.00 | 1.18 | 1.12 | 1.06 | 0.94 |
| 7 | Net | 2.00 | 2.35 | 2.23 | 2.12 | 1.88 |
| 8 | Price | 3.00 | 3.53 | 3.35 | 3.17 | 2.82 |
| 9 | | 4.00 | 4.70 | 4.47 | 4.23 | 3.76 |
| 10 | | 5.00 | 5.88 | 5.58 | 5.29 | 4.70 |
| 11 | | 6.00 | 7.05 | 6.70 | 6.35 | 5.64 |

## Options

Suppose that a formula in C54 referring to C24 is copied over the range C54:D56. There are four possible combinations for the reference in the new formulae:

☐ For a relative reference, both parts are changed when the formula is copied (e.g. C24 becomes C25, C26, D24, D25, D26).

☐ For an absolute reference, nothing changes (e.g. $C$24 stays as $C$24 no matter where it is copied).

☐ If the column is fixed, only the row number changes (e.g. $C24 becomes $C25, $C26, $C24, $C25, $C26).

☐ If the row is fixed, only the column letter changes (e.g. C$24 becomes C$24, C$24, D$24, D$24, D$24).

# Moving cells and ranges

To move the contents of a cell or range:

1 Click on the cell or drag over the range.

2 Press [Ctrl]+[X] to cut the highlighted area to the Clipboard (the cells are cleared).

3 Click on the cell that is to be the top left-hand corner of the range.

4 Press [Enter]. The contents of the cell or range appear in their new position.

As an alternative to copying the contents of cells (so that you have multiple copies), you can **move** the contents to a new location (clearing out the originals).

The principles are similar to those for copying but you will end up with a single copy of the original range in a new position.

## Tip

When a formula is moved, the cell references are not updated (unlike the effect when a formula is copied). If you want the references changed, you should copy the formula and then delete the original.

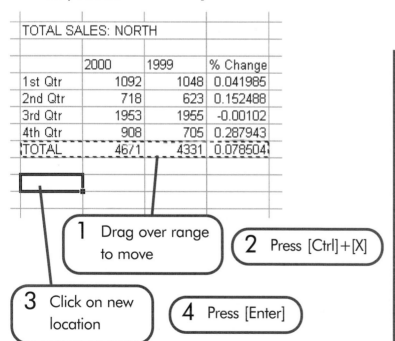

| TOTAL SALES: NORTH | | | |
|---|---|---|---|
| | 2000 | 1999 | % Change |
| 1st Qtr | 1092 | 1048 | 0.041985 |
| 2nd Qtr | 718 | 623 | 0.152488 |
| 3rd Qtr | 1953 | 1955 | -0.00102 |
| 4th Qtr | 908 | 705 | 0.287943 |
| TOTAL | 4671 | 4331 | 0.078504 |

1 Drag over range to move

2 Press [Ctrl]+[X]

3 Click on new location

4 Press [Enter]

## Take note

You can transpose data (change rows to columns and vice versa) using the TRANSPOSE function. For instructions on how to do this, activate Excel Help, type 'transpose' in the Answer Wizard and click on Search.

# Summary

❑ A formula can be copied to another cell, or copied over a range of cells. A range of cells can be copied to another location or repeated in multiple locations.

❑ Unless you specify otherwise, all cell references are up-dated so that they refer to the cells in the same **relative** positions.

❑ Cell references can be made **absolute** by putting $ in front of each part (e.g. $B$25 always refers to cell B25).

❑ Mixed cell references keep one part fixed while the other varies (e.g. $B25 always refers to column B but the row number may change; B$25 always refers to row 25 but the column may change).

❑ Cells and ranges can also be moved; the cell references in formulae are not updated after the move.

# 7 Number formats

# Applying number formats

Up until this point, numeric values have been displayed with the format that best suits them in each individual case: as whole numbers; with a limited number of decimal places; or using scientific format. This is the **General** format and you will usually want to change it in different parts of the worksheet. For example, monetary values will usually be displayed with exactly two decimal places; alternatively, you may want to round the results of calculations to the nearest whole number or a specific number of decimal places.

The format for a cell or range is altered using the Format|Cells command.

## Basic steps

1 Click on the cell to be formatted or mark a range of cells.

2 Select Cells from the Format menu, then click on the Number tab.

3 Choose the category that applies to the type of data being formatted.

4 Select the precise format, depending on category; e.g. for the Number category, select the number of decimal places, whether or not to use a thousands separator, and how to handle negative numbers.

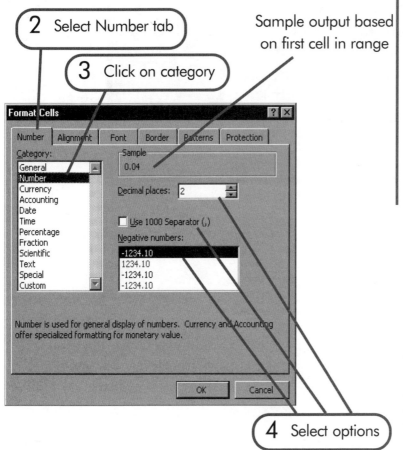

2 Select Number tab

Sample output based on first cell in range

3 Click on category

4 Select options

## Tip

Always save the worksheet before changing number formats, in case you apply the format to the wrong range.

# Format options

Number formats include integers (whole numbers) and various levels of decimal places.

Currency formats are similar to Number formats but insert a currency symbol at the front of the displayed number.

Date and Time formats provide several alternatives for the display of date and time values (see Chapter 8).

Percentage formats convert all values to percentages.

Fraction formats allow you to display fractions rather than decimals (e.g. $^{40}/_{47}$ instead of 0.851).

Scientific formats use the exponential style (see page 62).

Accounting formats are similar to Number formats but use a dash to represent zero values.

When you choose a number format, the Sample line in the dialog box shows you what the first highlighted cell will look like when it is displayed.

There is a wide range of possible formats built into the system. Some of these are described in more detail in the rest of this chapter.

| TOTAL SALES: NORTH | | | |
|---|---|---|---|
| | 2000 | 1999 | % Change |
| 1st Qtr | 1092 | 1048 | 4.20% |
| 2nd Qtr | 718 | 623 | 15.25% |
| 3rd Qtr | 1953 | 1955 | -0.10% |
| 4th Qtr | 908 | 705 | 28.79% |
| | | | |
| TOTAL | 4671 | 4331 | 7.85% |

Percentage format with 2 decimal places

Tip

Depending on the format you choose, Excel will add to the display value a monetary symbol (e.g. £), commas to separate thousands, % signs, and a minus sign or brackets for negative numbers. Although you can use these symbols when entering data, you cannot do so when entering formulae. Therefore, it is best not to enter the characters £ , % () yourself but let Excel apply them as appropriate. (Always indicate negative values with a − sign.)

# Decimal places

In most cases you will want to restrict the number of decimal places used in displayed values. The various formats on offer limit the number of figures after the decimal point.

- The **integer** format displays values as whole numbers (select the **Number** category with **0** decimal places).

- The various **floating point** formats (also in the **Number** category) give an exact number of decimal places; if necessary, extra 0s are added at the end to pad out the number.

- The **Percentage** format can be a bit confusing; formatting 0.175 as a percentage results in a display of **17.5%**.

- The **Currency** format works like a floating point value but inserts a currency symbol (e.g. £).

The Custom format gives you complete control over the display style (see page 68). (Note that values are stored with 15 significant figures, which includes all figures before and after the decimal point.)

**Tip**

Do not use more decimal places than are reasonable or necessary. For instance, with monetary values there is rarely a need for more than two decimal places.

**Take note**

The General format displays up to nine decimal places.

---

**Take note**

There are several buttons on the toolbar that can be used to apply a particular type of format to a marked range.

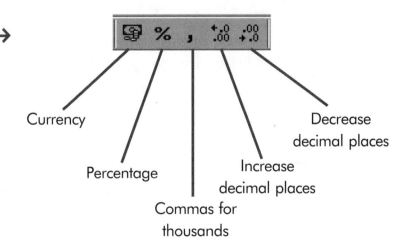

Currency

Percentage

Commas for thousands

Increase decimal places

Decrease decimal places

# Stored and displayed values

## Precision as displayed

Sometimes you want the stored value to match the displayed value: for example, most calculations involving money will need the result stored to the nearest penny and not with a dozen decimal places!

The Tools | Options | Calculation | Precision As Displayed option permanently changes stored values so that they match the displayed amounts.

When the General format is applied, the displayed value will have as many decimal places as are necessary for the value on screen to match that stored in memory (providing the column is wide enough). The value in any cell, whether entered directly or calculated from a formula, is stored in memory with 15 significant figures.

However, as soon as a different format is applied, with the number of decimal places limited, the value will be rounded for the display. For example, with an integer display format, any value ending in .5 or more will be rounded **up** to the next whole number while those less than .5 are rounded **down**. Thus 3.5, 3.501 and 3.95 are all rounded up to 4 but 3.01, 3.45 and 3.49995 are all rounded down to 3.

The most important point is that all calculations use the **stored** value, rather than the **displayed** value. This can lead to some surprising results, even when there is no division involved.

|   | Actual value | Integer display |   |
|---|---|---|---|
| A | 2.45 | 2 |   |
| B | 2.35 | 2 |   |
| C = A + B | 4.8 | 5 | 2 + 2 = 5 ! |
| D = C * 3 | 14.4 | 14 | 5 * 3 = 14 ! |

# The Currency format

The Currency format inserts a currency symbol in front of each value. You can choose either the default symbol (which will depend on the regional settings set up within Windows on your computer) or some other symbol from the drop-down list.

Click to choose currency
symbol from drop-down list

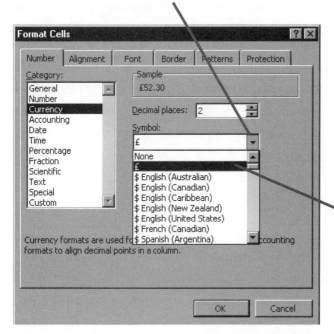

Default currency
symbol shown at
top of list

Empty square box
indicates euro symbol
not supported

When you mark a part of the worksheet with the default Currency format you may find that the values are displayed with $ at the front rather than £ (or other local currency). In this case, Windows is not set up for UK (or other national) use; the currency symbol is a function of Windows, rather than Excel 2000.

To change the symbol, double-click on the Regional Settings icon in the Windows Control Panel (selected from the Settings group in the Start menu). Then click on the Currency tab, enter the £ sign (or other symbol) as the Currency Symbol and click on OK. As soon as you get back to Excel, the display will be updated.

Type symbol here

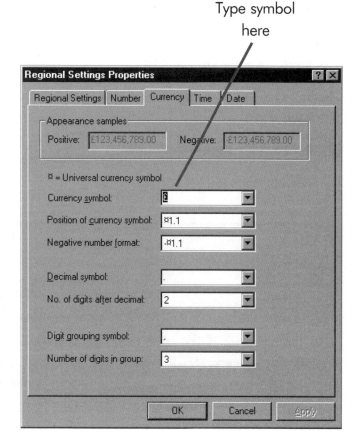

# Scientific format

The **Scientific** format is used for very large and very small numbers, where the scale of the number makes it difficult to comprehend if written as a normal decimal. This format, which is most commonly found in scientific applications, is also referred to as the **exponential** format.

The format represents numbers in the form:

**x.xxE±yy**

The first part (x.xx) is a number in the range 1.00 to 9.99. The last part (yy) is a power of ten by which the number must be multiplied to get the required value; this is the **exponent**. For example:

**52.3 = 5.23 x 10 = 5.23E+01**

**523 = 5.23 x 10$^2$ = 5.23E+02**

**5230 = 5.23 x 10$^3$ = 5.23E+03**

There is a special case when the number is already in the range 1 to 9.99:

**5.23 = 5.23 x 10$^0$ = 5.23E+00**

## Effects

- ☐ Multiplying a number by 10 increases the exponent by 1; dividing by 10 reduces the exponent by 1.

  e.g. **6.98E+04 x 10 = 6.98E+05**

  **6.98E+04 / 10 = 6.98E+03**

- ☐ When two numbers are multiplied together the parts on the left are multiplied and the exponents are added.

  e.g. **2E+02 x 3E+05 = 6E+07**

- ☐ When one number is divided by another, the division is carried out on the numbers on the left and the second exponent is subtracted from the first.

  e.g. **8E+03 / 2E+02 = 4E+01**

## Take note

If you enter a value in Scientific form, Excel uses that format for the cell, even if the value is not particularly large or small. For example, if you enter '5.2e1' it is displayed as '5.20E+01' while '523e34' appears as '5.23E+36'.

The exponent can also be negative, indicating that the value is to be divided by 10 to a given power. For example:

$$0.523 = 5.23 / 10 = 5.23E{-}01$$

$$0.0523 = 5.23 / 10^2 = 5.23E{-}02$$

Don't get confused by this minus sign; these values are positive. A **value** is only negative if there is a minus sign on the left of the main number. For example:

$$-523 = -5.23 \times 10^2 = -5.23E{+}02$$

$$-0.0523 = -5.23 \times 10^{-2} = -5.23E{-}02$$

|    | A | B | C | D | E |
|----|---|---|---|---|---|
| 1  |   |   |   |   |   |
| 2  |   |   | General | Decimal (2 dp) | Scientific |
| 3  |   |   |   |   |   |
| 4  |   | 5.23 * 100000000 | 523000000 | 523000000.00 | 5.23E+08 |
| 5  |   | 5.23 * 100 | 523 | 523.00 | 5.23E+02 |
| 6  |   | 5.23 * 10 | 52.3 | 52.30 | 5.23E+01 |
| 7  |   | 5.23 | 5.23 | 5.23 | 5.23E+00 |
| 8  |   | 5.23 /10 | 0.523 | 0.52 | 5.23E-01 |
| 9  |   | 5.23 /100 | 0.0523 | 0.05 | 5.23E-02 |
| 10 |   | 5.23 / 100000000 | 5.23E-08 | 0.00 | 5.23E-08 |
| 11 |   |   |   |   |   |
| 12 |   | -5.23 * 100000000 | -523000000 | -523000000.00 | -5.23E+08 |
| 13 |   | -5.23 * 100 | -523 | -523.00 | -5.23E+02 |
| 14 |   | -5.23 * 10 | -52.3 | -52.30 | -5.23E+01 |
| 15 |   | -5.23 | -5.23 | -5.23 | -5.23E+00 |
| 16 |   | -5.23 /10 | -0.523 | -0.52 | -5.23E-01 |
| 17 |   | -5.23 /100 | -0.0523 | -0.05 | -5.23E-02 |
| 18 |   | -5.23 / 100000000 | -5.23E-08 | 0.00 | -5.23E-08 |
| 19 |   |   |   |   |   |

# Summary

❏ By default, all cells are formatted with the General format, which applies the most suitable display style in each case.

❏ The format for a cell or range is changed with the Format | Cells command.

❏ Numbers are stored with 15 significant figures of accuracy; there are bound to be slight inaccuracies in results, particularly when divisions occur; these will not usually be a problem.

❏ Calculations use the stored values, not the displayed values. The stored values can be changed to match the displayed values with Tools | Options | Calculation | Precision As Displayed (which applies to the whole file).

❏ Formats with a fixed number of decimal places include Integer, Floating Point, Percentage, Currency and Accountancy.

❏ The Scientific format is normally used for very large and very small numbers.

# 8 Other formats

# Dates and times

Excel can handle dates and times in calculations. It does this by storing any date or time as a numeric code, rather than as text.

Dates are stored as integers, representing the number of days since 30th December 1899. For example, 36526 represents 1st January 2000.

If you enter a date in the General format, Excel displays it in the form dd/mm/yy. If this is then copied to another cell and formatted as an integer, the number that represents that date will be shown. Similarly, an integer formatted as a date will show in date format provided it is within the permissible range.

## Limits

☐ The earliest date you should use is 01/03/1900, represented by the value 61.

☐ The latest date recognised by Excel is 31/12/9999, represented by 2,958,465.

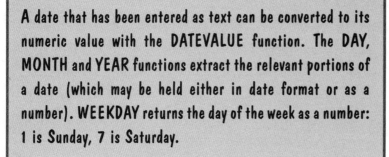

| | A | B | C | D | E |
|---|---|---|---|---|---|
| 1 | | | | | |
| 2 | | Date | 07/05/90 | | |
| 3 | | Date value | 33000 | | =C2, formatted as a number |
| 4 | | | | | |
| 5 | | Time | 4:00 AM | | |
| 6 | | Time value | 0.17 | | =C5, formatted as a number |
| 7 | | | | | |
| 8 | | Value | 37025.96 | | |
| 9 | | Date & Time | 14/05/2001 23:02 | | =C8, formatted as dd/mm/yyyy hh:mm |
| 10 | | | | | |
| 11 | | | | | |

**Take note**

**The values for dates before March 1900 are wrong, as Excel incorrectly treats 1900 as a leap year.**

**Tip**

**A date that has been entered as text can be converted to its numeric value with the DATEVALUE function. The DAY, MONTH and YEAR functions extract the relevant portions of a date (which may be held either in date format or as a number). WEEKDAY returns the day of the week as a number: 1 is Sunday, 7 is Saturday.**

**Take note**

**Earlier versions of Excel had a limit for dates of 31/12/2078.**

The following functions can be used to derive values from the system clock:

☐ TODAY returns the current date.

☐ NOW returns the current date and time.

In a similar way, time of day is stored as a number in the range 0 to 1, with the value representing the portion of the day that has elapsed. So 6 a.m. is represented by 0.25, midday is 0.5 and midnight is 0.

Numbers and times (including AM and PM if required) can be interchanged by applying numeric or time formats.

You can also combine a date and time; the part to the left of the decimal place represents the date, that to the right represents the time. For instance, the value 36526.25 represents 1-Jan-2000 6:00 AM.

## Tip

**Use NOW on sheets that are to be printed out. The current date and time are updated whenever the sheet is loaded or recalculated.**

Defaults to American format (mm/dd/yy) – use Custom format for dd/mm/yyyy

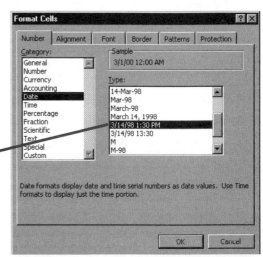

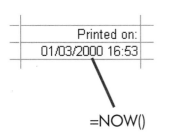

Printed on:
01/03/2000 16:53

=NOW()

## Take note

**A time entered as text is converted to a numeric value with TIMEVALUE. The HOUR, MINUTE and SECOND functions extract the relevant integers from a time that is held as a numeric value.**

# Custom formats

You can create your own customised formats if none of those supplied by Excel is quite right. Select Format|Cells and click on the Custom tab. Either choose one of the existing formats and edit it, or create your own format in the Type box.

The format consists of up to four sections, separated by semi-colons:

- The format for positive numbers

- The format for negative numbers

- The format for zero

- The format for text entered in the cell

Each part of the format is made up of a series of special codes. In particular, you can use symbols such as £ and %, or a full stop as the decimal point. Negative values should be preceded or followed by a minus sign, or enclosed in brackets. The digits in the number are represented by #, 0 or ? symbols.

If any part of the format is omitted, the display is blank for corresponding values.

## Take note

Custom date and time formats can be created using d, m, y, h, m and s components. The Custom category has several alternatives, which can be further customised.

## Digits

The format characters for digits have the following meaning:

- ☐ A digit represented by # will not be displayed if it is zero and either at the beginning of the number or in the last decimal place.

- ☐ A digit represented by 0 is always displayed, even when zero.

- ☐ A ? after the decimal point displays a space if the digit is zero and at the end of the number (so the decimal points will still line up).

If there are more digits to the right of the decimal place than there are format characters, the number is rounded; if there are insufficient format characters to the left, the complete number is shown anyway.

# Text

- You can include fixed or variable text in any part of the format.

- Text included in number formats must always be in double quotes (").

- An @ symbol is replaced by the actual text entered in the cell.

## Take note

You can get any value to show in a different colour by putting the colour name in square brackets in front of the format. For example, [Red] in front of the second part of the format results in negative values being displayed in red on the screen.

The format in the illustration below is as follows:

**£0.00;[Red]-£0.00;"Nil";"Invalid: "@**

This is interpreted as follows:

- Positive numbers have a leading £ sign, at least one digit before the decimal point and always two decimal places.

- Negative numbers have a minus sign and are shown in red.

- Zero values are shown as the text 'Nil'.

- Text entries are displayed as the word 'Invalid:' followed by a space and the actual text entered.

For more information on the options available, search the Answer Wizard for 'Create a custom number format' and then click on one of the links at the bottom of the topic.

Sample output based on first cell in range

Enter custom format codes here

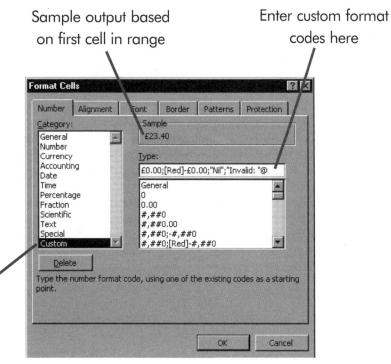

New format will be added to this category

69

# Summary

❑ Dates are stored as whole numbers, counting from 31/12/1899 up to 31/12/9999 (accurate from March 1900 only).

❑ Times are stored as decimals in the range 0 to 1, representing the proportion of the day that has elapsed.

❑ A single floating point number can represent a combined date and time.

❑ Customised display formats can be designed, consisting of four parts: positive numbers, negative numbers, zero, text.

❑ Customised formats can also be created for dates and times, using d, m, y, h, m and s components.

# 9 Formatting worksheets

# Column width and row height

Entering values and formulae is only the start of using a worksheet. Usually, you will be aiming to produce some type of report from the worksheet or, at the very least, will want to improve the layout of the sheet for your own benefit.

The first stage is to change the widths of the columns to make them more suitable for the data they contain. By default, each column starts with a column width of about nine numeric characters. You can change this default – so that all columns take this new width – or you can adjust individual columns.

## Take note

When you insert a new cell, it is given the width of the column immediately to the left, not the width of the current column.

Column width is given in terms of the average number of characters in the standard font

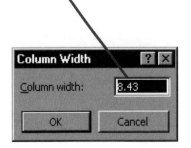

| Column Width | ? X |
|---|---|
| Column width: | 8.43 |
| OK | Cancel |

## Width options

- [ ] Select Format | Column | Standard Width to set a new default width.

- [ ] Click on a cell or mark a range and then select Format | Column | Width to change the width of one or more columns.

- [ ] Select Format | Column | AutoFit Selection to make the width of one or more columns automatically adjust to fit the longest item of data in each case.

- [ ] Use the Format Painter to copy the width of one column to another (see page 89).

## Take note

If a cell is filled with # characters, the column is not wide enough to display the numeric value held in the cell. Increasing the width will allow the number to be shown again.

# Height options

□ Select Format | Row | Height to change the height of a single row or a highlighted series of rows.

□ Select Format | Row | AutoFit to make the height of the rows adjust to fit their contents.

In a similar way to the width, you can adjust the height of each row. This will be necessary if you change the fonts, use multi-line text, or simply want to put a bigger gap between sections of the worksheet.

Row height is given in points; there are 72 points per inch. The standard font uses 10-point text.

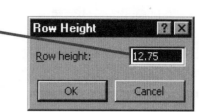

## Shortcuts

● The quickest way to change the width of a single column is to drag the right-hand edge of the column border (next to the column letter). To make a column fit the widest item of data in that column, double-click on the column border.

● The easiest way to change the height of a row is to drag the bottom edge of the row border (immediately below the row number).

Double-click on border to make column fit widest item in column B

Drag here to change width of column A

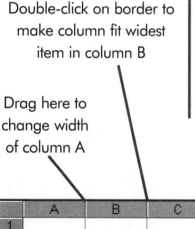

Drag here to change height of row 4

## Take note

If you change the font used for a cell (see page 84), the row height is adjusted to suit the new font. Similarly, if text is formatted to be multi-line, any row that contains a cell where the text has been split over more than one line will expand to fit the text.

# Alignment

When data is first entered, text is placed on the left of the cell and numbers line up on the right. Numbers can be tidied up by applying a suitable format: for example, a fixed number of decimal places. For most purposes this is satisfactory but there are times when you need the text to be aligned to the right of the cell or the numbers on the left.

The Format|Cells command has an Alignment tab that allows you to change the position of data in any cell. As a shortcut, four of the buttons on the toolbar can be used to apply a new alignment to the range that is currently highlighted.

The Vertical options allow you to decide whether the text is at the top, bottom or middle of the row. You can also display text at an angle.

To change the alignment of a cell or range:

1 Mark the cell or range to be re-aligned.

2 Select Cells from the Format menu.

3 Click on the Alignment tab.

4 Choose Left, Center or Right alignment.

Or:

1 Mark the cell or range to be re-aligned.

2 Click on the appropriate button on the toolbar.

| This | This | This |
|------|------|------|
| text | text | text |
| is | is | is |
| left | centred | right |
| aligned | | aligned |

Left aligned    Centred    Right aligned

Merge and Center

Click to change angle

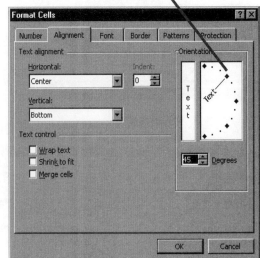

# Basic steps

To centre a piece of text over more than one column:

1 Type the text into the left-hand column.

2 Mark a range, starting with the text cell and extending over the cells in which the text is to be centred. (All cells in the range must be empty.)

3 Select Format | Cells and choose Center Across Selection from the Horizontal list on the Alignment tab.

You can also use the Merge and Center button on the toolbar but this has a more permanent effect, merging the selected cells into a single cell.

Text can spread over more than one column or row.

● If you type text into a cell that is too narrow, and the cell to the right is empty, the text will spread over both columns on the display.

● Text can be **centred** over a group of cells, providing these are all blank, by setting the Horizontal alignment to Center Across Selection.

● Text can be made to **wrap** over multiple lines within a cell, using the Wrap Text option from the Alignment tab. Any words that will not fit on one line are carried over to the next line and the height of the row adjusts to take all the text.

● Text that has been wrapped in a cell can be**justified**, so that there is a straight right-hand margin; use the Justify option from the Horizontal drop-down list.

Center Across Selection

| | B2 | ▼ | = | TOTAL SALES: NORTH | |
|---|---|---|---|---|---|
| | A | B | C | D | E |
| 1 | | | | | |
| 2 | | | TOTAL SALES: NORTH | | |
| 3 | | | | | |
| 4 | | | 2000 | 1999 | % Change |
| 5 | | 1st Qtr | 1092 | 1048 | 4.20% |
| 6 | | 2nd Qtr | 718 | 623 | 15.25% |
| 7 | | 3rd Qtr | 1953 | 1955 | -0.10% |
| 8 | | 4th Qtr | 908 | 705 | 28.79% |

## Take note

Text will only spread into the next column or be centred over columns if the neighbouring cells are completely empty. Clearing them by pressing the space bar is not enough; use Edit | Clear | All.

Although text may be displayed in several columns, it is still stored in its original cell as far as Excel is concerned.

# Inserting rows and columns

You should always design the layout of the worksheet before you start to put anything on the computer but, inevitably, there will be times when you don't get it right first time. You can delete or move the contents of cells without any difficulty and you may also need to insert or delete rows or columns.

New rows are inserted above the current row, new columns to the left of the current column, using the Insert menu.

Insert rows

Insert columns

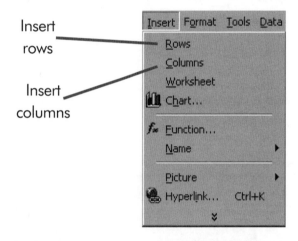

To insert a row or column:

1 Click on a cell.

2 Select Rows or Columns from the Insert menu.

For Rows, the new row is inserted above the current row; for Columns, the new column is inserted to the left of the current column.

To insert more than one row or column, highlight the required number of cells. For instance, to insert three blank rows, start by marking a range that covers three existing rows.

## Take note

All new columns have the same width and format as the column to the left.

All formulae are updated so that they still relate to the same cells as before (regardless of whether the references were relative or absolute).

## Tip

To insert a row or column quickly, right-click on the row number or column letter and select Insert from the pop-up menu. To insert several rows or columns, highlight the required number of rows or columns before right-clicking.

# Deleting rows and columns

## Basic steps

To delete a row or column:

1 Mark a range that covers all the rows or columns to be deleted.

2 Select Delete from the Edit menu; the Delete dialog box appears.

3 Click on Entire Row to delete one or more rows, Entire Column for the columns.

Rows and columns are erased from the worksheet with frightening simplicity. The Edit|Delete command lets you cut out any section of the sheet.

Delete rows

Delete columns

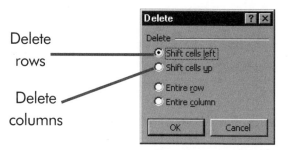

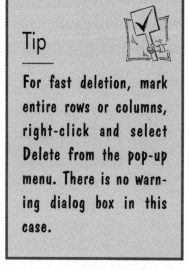

## Tip

For fast deletion, mark entire rows or columns, right-click and select Delete from the pop-up menu. There is no warning dialog box in this case.

## Tip

Always save the worksheet with [Ctrl]+ [S] before deleting anything; it is very easy to make mistakes and deletions cannot always be undone.

## Take note

After a deletion, all rows and columns are renumbered and all formulae are revised so that they still refer to the original cells. If you delete a row or column that is part of a range reference, the formula will adjust; however, if you delete the whole of a range from a reference or an individual cell that is referenced, the result of the formula will be #REF! and the formula will have to be amended.

# Inserting and deleting cells

You can achieve most effects by inserting and deleting rows and columns, moving or copying ranges, or combining these operations. Sometimes it is a useful shortcut to be able to insert or delete **ranges** of cells.

When you insert cells, all cells to the right or below move left or down to make space for them. The contents of other rows and columns are not affected.

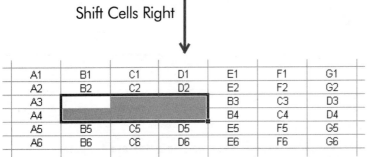

Shift Cells Right

Move cells in selected rows to the right

Move cells in selected columns down

## Inserting

To insert a range of cells:

1 Mark a range of cells. The top left-hand corner of the range determines the insertion point; the size of the range determines how much of the sheet will be affected and how many cells will be inserted.

2 Select Cells from the hidden portion of the Insert menu. (Click on the arrows at the bottom of the menu to show all the options.)

3 Click on Shift Cells Right or Shift Cells Down, depending on the direction you want the range to move.

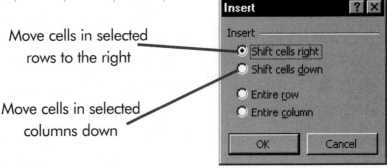

# Deleting

To delete a range of cells:

**1** Mark a range of cells to be deleted.

**2** Select Delete from the Edit menu.

**3** Click on Shift Cells Left or Shift Cells Up, depending on how you want to fill the gap.

Inserting and deleting cells requires more thought than other, similar operations and most of the time you will stick to column and row actions. However, the cell operations are particularly useful where a group of values are in the wrong row or column.

Move cells in selected rows to the left

Move cells in selected columns up

**Delete**                          ? ×

Delete

○ Shift cells left
◉ Shift cells up

○ Entire row
○ Entire column

OK        Cancel

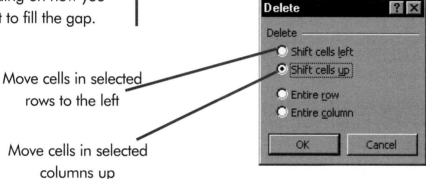

| | | | | | |
|---|---|---|---|---|---|
| January | 124 | | January | 124 | |
| February | 354 | | February | 354 | |
| March | 276 | | March | 276 | |
| April | 45 | **Shift** | April | 45 | |
| May | 2890 | **Cells** | May | 2890 | |
| June | 46 | | June | 46 | |
| July | 348 | **Up** | July | 348 | |
| August | 348 | → | August | 2907 | |
| September | 348 | | September | 3591 | |
| October | 2907 | | October | 397 | |
| November | 3591 | | November | 226 | |
| December | 397 | | December | 623 | |
| | 226 | | | | |
| | 623 | | | | |

Two cells deleted, cells below shifted up to fill gap

# Fixing titles

On large worksheets, you may need to be able to see the titles at the top of the sheet, or the row headings on the left, when you are working with data at some distant point. You can do this by **freezing** the titles.

The Window|Freeze Panes command allows you to fix the rows above the current cell so that they will no longer scroll out of view. However, if you move the cursor to the right, the rows will still scroll right. Similarly, the columns to the left of the current cell are fixed and will only scroll up and down.

To free the titles again, select Window|Unfreeze Panes.

To freeze the titles:

1 Click on the cell in the top-left corner of the area that is to move freely (cell C5 in the example).

2 Select Window|Freeze Panes.

You can move anywhere on the sheet (including the title areas) but the titles are always visible. In the example, columns A and B are fixed, as are rows 1 to 4.

Completely fixed

Scrolls horizontally

|  | A | B | E | F | G | H |
|---|---|---|---|---|---|---|
| 1 |  |  |  |  |  |  |
| 2 |  |  |  | Order Summary |  |  |
| 3 |  |  |  |  |  |  |
| 4 |  | No. | Company | Reference | Qty | Unit Price |
| 38 |  | 38 | Southbury Supplies | KB-995/02 | 23 | 2.87 |
| 39 |  | 39 | Southbury Supplies | FB-230/03 | 401 | 0.45 |
| 40 |  | 40 | ABT Ltd | KB-995/02 | 8 | 2.87 |
| 41 |  | 41 | Westwood Enterprises | RT9-405-356 | 12 | 12.45 |
| 42 |  | 42 | Southbury Supplies | KB-995/02 | 54 | 2.87 |
| 43 |  | 43 | Southbury Supplies | SB-087/00 | 340 | 80.03 |
| 44 |  | 44 | ABT Ltd | AFT88/2/W/a | 7 | 17.95 |
| 45 |  |  |  |  |  |  |
| 46 |  |  |  |  |  |  |
| 47 |  |  |  |  |  |  |

Scrolls normally

Scrolls vertically

## Tip

**To fix rows only, put the cursor in column A; to fix columns only, put the cursor in row 1.**

## Take note

**The Window|Split command divides the sheet into two or four areas, in a similar way, but any of these can be scrolled independently of the others.**

# Protecting data

1 Mark the cells in which data entry is to be allowed. (Click on a column letter or row number to mark a whole column or row.)

2 Select Format | Cells, click on the Protection Tab and clear the Locked box.

3 Repeat for other ranges not to be protected.

4 Select Tools | Protection | Protect Sheet. Enter a password if required (make sure Caps Lock is off). Click on OK.

Clear the protection with Tools | Protection | Unprotect Sheet.

Much of the sheet will contain data that is to be derived from formulae and therefore must not be changed directly. You can protect the worksheet against alterations, so that data is entered only in certain areas.

The Tools menu contains an option to protect the entire sheet against change. Before choosing this option, you must identify those areas of the sheet where changes are to be allowed. Users of the sheet will then not be able to overwrite data accidentally.

If you apply a password, users will have to enter the correct password before any changes can be made.

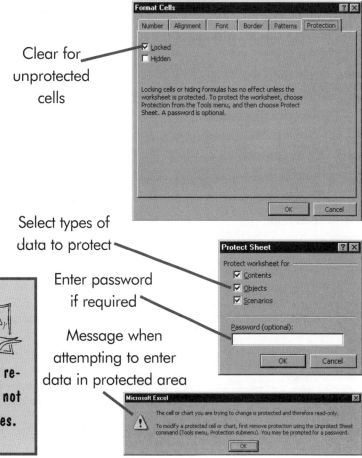

Clear for unprotected cells

Select types of data to protect

Enter password if required

Message when attempting to enter data in protected area

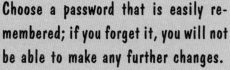

## Take note

Choose a password that is easily remembered; if you forget it, you will not be able to make any further changes.

81

# Summary

- The width of any column can be changed with the Format |Column command or by dragging the divider between column letters.

- The height of any row is changed with Format|Row or by dragging the divider between row numbers.

- Text can be aligned to the left or right of the cell, or centred within the cell or across a series of cells.

- New rows or columns can be inserted with the Insert menu, or deleted with the Edit |Delete command.

- Blocks of cells can also be inserted or deleted (though moving blocks is preferable).

- Titles can be fixed with the Window | Freeze Panes command, so that they are always visible, no matter where you are in the sheet.

- The worksheet can be protected against change with Tools |Protection|Protect Sheet. Areas where data entry is to be allowed must be marked first with Format | Cells | Protection.

# 10 Cosmetics

# Changing fonts

The **font** is the style of text used to display the contents of cells (both text and numeric values). A font is defined by the following characteristics:

- The typeface (e.g. Arial, Times and Courier)

- The point size (e.g. 8 point, 10 point and 12 point)

- The attributes (e.g. **bold**, *italic* and underline)

Fonts are applied to cells and ranges in a similar way to other characteristics, such as alignment. Although you can use the Font tab from the Format|Cells command, the easiest way is to use the buttons on the toolbar.

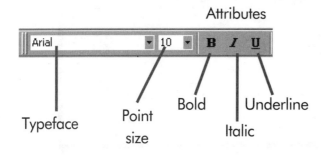

Attributes

Typeface    Point size    Bold    Italic    Underline

## Basic steps

To change the font for cells:

1 Select the cell or range to which the new font is to be applied.

2 Click on the arrow to the right of the typeface box on the toolbar and click on the required typeface from the drop-down list.

3 In a similar way, select the point size (or simply type the size directly into the Point Size box).

4 Click on the bold, italic or underline buttons to change the attributes. Each time you click a button, the attribute is turned on or off. Any combination of at-tributes is allowed. When an attribute has been turned on, the corresponding button is shown in paler grey.

The default font is 10-point Arial, with no attributes set.

## Basic steps

To change the font for a group of characters:

1 Double-click on the cell containing the text (for text centred across columns, the left-hand cell of the range).

2 Drag the pointer over the characters to be changed, highlighting them.

3 Select the typeface, size and attributes, as before.

The following keys are shortcuts for the attributes:

[Ctrl]+[B]     Bold

[Ctrl]+[I]     Italic

[Ctrl]+[U]     Underline

For cells formatted as numbers or dates, the font applies to all the characters in the cell. For text cells, however, you can format individual characters and groups of characters. This allows you to produce a mixture of fonts within a cell and is particularly useful for headings.

| | A | B | C | D | E | |
|---|---|---|---|---|---|---|
| 1 | | | | | | |
| 2 | | TOTAL SALES: NORTH | | | | |
| 3 | | | | | | |
| 4 | | | 2000 | 1999 | % Change | |
| 5 | | 1st Qtr | 1092 | 1048 | 4.20% | |
| 6 | | 2nd Qtr | 718 | 623 | 15.25% | |
| 7 | | 3rd Qtr | 1953 | 1955 | -0.10% | |
| 8 | | 4th Qtr | 908 | 705 | 28.79% | |
| 9 | | | | | | |
| 10 | | | | | | |
| 11 | | TOTAL | 4671 | 4331 | 7.85% | |
| 12 | | | | | | |

22 point bold    14 point bold    10 point right-aligned

# Borders, patterns and colours

For further enhancement of your work, and to highlight particular blocks of data or subdivide complicated tables, Excel provides a range of features for drawing boxes, shading cells and changing the colours.

Click here to apply     Click here to change

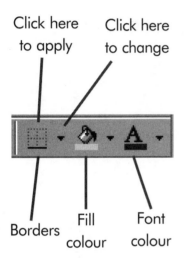

Borders    Fill colour    Font colour

Click to show options

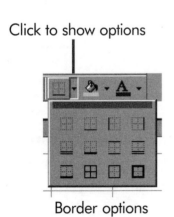

Border options

## Options

There are two ways of changing these features for the current cell or a highlighted range:

☐ Select the Format | Cells command, then click on the Border, Patterns or Font tab.

☐ Click on the arrows to the right of the borders, fill colour and font colour buttons on the toolbar, then select from the drop-down lists.

When a border, colour or pattern has been chosen, it can be applied to further cells or ranges by selecting the area to be changed and clicking on the appropriate button again.

## Tip

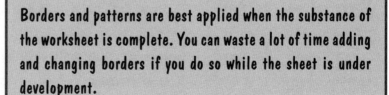

These buttons can be adding to the Formatting toolbar by clicking on the »button, then on Add Or Remove Buttons, and finally on the required buttons.

## Tip

Borders and patterns are best applied when the substance of the worksheet is complete. You can waste a lot of time adding and changing borders if you do so while the sheet is under development.

Borders, patterns and colours can be applied to individual cells or ranges.

● To draw a border around a block of cells, highlight the entire block, then choose the border.

● To divide columns with vertical lines, mark each column separately and apply a border on the right (or left).

● To box individual cells, each cell must be given its own border.

The background colour is applied to whole cells. In the same way as for fonts, the text colour can be changed for individual characters in a text cell but must be applied to the entire cell for numbers and dates.

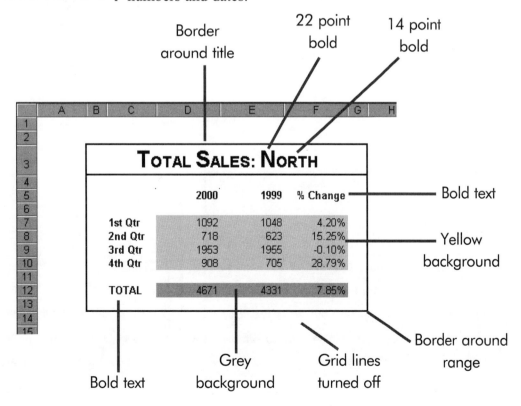

87

# Hiding rows and columns

The results produced on worksheets often require a series of steps, with one or more intermediate values. These extra cells may clutter the display and be of no interest in themselves, once the sheet is working satisfactorily. Therefore the unwanted values can be placed in separate rows and columns, which can then be **hidden**.

The effect of hiding a row or column is purely that it does not appear on the display or in printouts; the formulae in hidden rows and columns still work in exactly the same way as before and there is no effect on the results.

Columns F
and G hidden

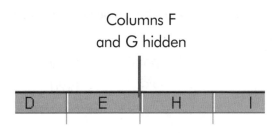

**To hide rows or columns:**

1 Mark a range that covers at least one cell in each of the rows or columns to be hidden.

2 Select Format | Row | Hide or Format | Column | Hide.

**To redisplay rows or columns:**

1 Click on the border between adjacent cells (where the row or column will reappear).

2 Select Format | Row | Unhide or Format | Column | Unhide.

## Take note

The title bar, toolbars and status bar can be hidden (or redisplayed) using View | Full Screen. The Row & Column Headers option in the View tab of the Tools | Options command hides the row letters and column numbers.

## Tip

You can tell when there are hidden rows or columns on a worksheet because there will be a jump in the row numbers or column letters.

# Copying formats

To copy a format:

**1** Click on the cell whose format is to be copied.

**2** Click on the Format Painter button.

**3** Mark the range that is to receive the new format.

When the mouse button is released, the new format is applied to all the high-lighted cells, replacing whatever was there before.

You can undo mistakes in formatting with [Ctrl]+[Z].

Once you have created a display format for one cell, you can easily copy this to any other range on the worksheet using the Format Painter. This will apply the same number/text format, alignment, font, border, pattern and colour to all selected cells.

You can also copy the format of an entire row or column. If you mark a row by clicking on the row number, click on the Format Painter button and then click on another row number (or drag over several rows), the format will be copied, including the row height. Similarly, you can use the Format Painter to copy the format for a column, including column width.

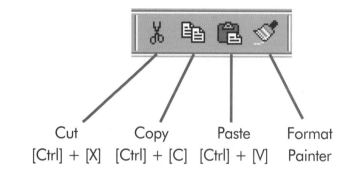

Cut
[Ctrl] + [X]

Copy
[Ctrl] + [C]

Paste
[Ctrl] + [V]

Format
Painter

Tip

To copy the format to several ranges, double-click on the Format Painter button. Mark the required ranges, then click the button again.

Take note

You can also copy several formats from one range to another, providing the ranges have a similar layout. For example, the formats for the first row of the original block is copied to the first row of the new block, the format for the first column is copied to the corresponding column on the new block, and so on. However, the result may not always be as you expect, so always save the worksheet first.

# Format styles

For simple sheets and one-off applications, the ability to copy formats between cells is all you need. For more complex applications, however, it is useful to give names to the format combinations you use.

A **style** is a combination of number/text format, alignment, font, border, pattern, colour and protection status. All you have to do is give the style a name, and this can be applied to any other range in the worksheet.

The use of styles is particularly important when you are creating a series of worksheets or wish to devise a company standard to be used by a number of people.

To create a style:

1 Apply the necessary formatting to an individual cell.

2 With the cell highlighted, select Format | Style and enter a new name in the Style box.

3 You can restrict the style to just some of the formatting features. For instance, you may set up a style for everything except the number format; all cells with this style will have the same appearance (font, alignment etc.) but can have different number formats.

4 Click on OK when the style is complete or Cancel to abandon.

The new style can now be applied to other cells or ranges.

Enter new style name

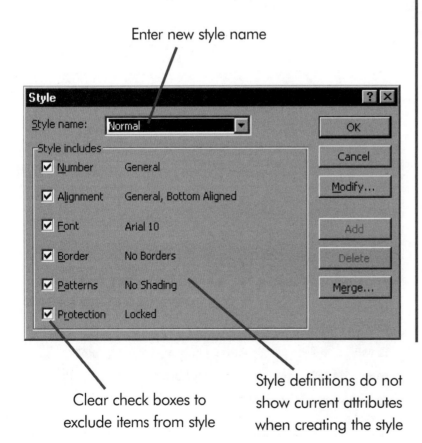

Clear check boxes to exclude items from style

Style definitions do not show current attributes when creating the style

When a style has been defined, you can use it as follows:

- To apply a style to a range of cells, highlight the range and then click on the required style from the Style box in the Format | Style window. Any existing formatting on the cells is lost.

- After applying a style, individual formatting elements can be overridden for selected cells (for instance, you can change the colour of a cell but the other style elements stay the same).

- To change a style, select Format | Style, choose the style from the drop-down list and click on Modify. Then update any element of the style. When you click on OK, all cells that have this style are updated (except where the style has been overridden by manual changes).

- To delete a style, select Format | Style, choose the style and click on Delete. Any cells with this style have the style removed (effectively, they are given the Normal style) but any later formatting that was added still applies.

Style box added to Formatting toolbar

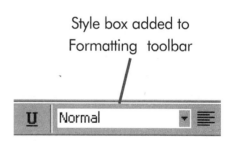

# Summary

❑ The **font** is the style of the text, consisting of typeface, point size and attributes (bold, italic, underline).

❑ Any font can be applied to a cell and, in text cells, individual characters can be given different fonts. Each numeric or date cell can have only one font.

❑ Borders can be drawn around cells and ranges, which can also be given a background of a different pattern or colour.

❑ In text cells, individual characters can be different colours; each numeric or date cell can have only one colour.

❑ Rows and columns can be hidden from view but their formulae will still be calculated in the usual way.

❑ The grid lines, toolbars and borders can also be hidden.

❑ The Format Painter is used to copy the format of a cell to other cells; features copied include the number format, alignment, font, border, pattern, colour and protection status.

❑ Formats can be named to produce **styles**. A named style can be applied to any cell or range.

# 11 Workbooks

# Multiple worksheets

So far, we have considered just a single worksheet. Excel allows you to have several worksheets in a single file, which is referred to as a **workbook**. A workbook may also contain chart sheets, where you can display graphs and charts of the data from your worksheets.

Whenever you save the file, **all** sheets in the workbook will be saved together. Similarly, loading a file loads into memory **all** the sheets in the workbook.

The sheets are shown in the sheet tabs at the bottom of the window.

The sheets in a workbook can be of two different types:

☐ Worksheets, for the entry of data and formulae and the calculation of results

☐ Chart sheets, for the display of graphs and charts (see page 116).

Current sheet

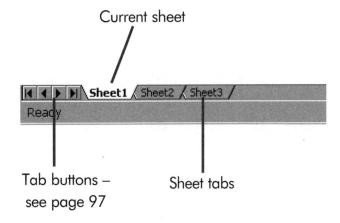

Tab buttons –
see page 97

Sheet tabs

## Take note

Previous versions of Excel allowed Visual Basic sheets and Dialog sheets. These are now accessed with the Visual Basic Editor – see page 142.

## Tip

Only include worksheets in a workbook if there is going to be some beneficial effect from doing so. For instance, if data from one sheet is used on another sheet or a series of sheets are always printed together in a report, then it is worth putting them all in the same workbook. However, if a number of worksheets are similar but not related in any other way, they are probably better saved in separate files; otherwise you are just making matters more complicated unnecessarily.

# Basic steps

To rename a sheet in a workbook:

**1** Double-click on the sheet tab at the bottom of the window.

**2** Enter a new name in the sheet tab; the name can use any characters (maximum length 31), including spaces.

**3** Click on OK. The new name is shown in the sheet tab, which expands to show the full name.

You can also rename sheets with Format│Sheet│Rename.

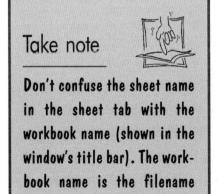
Each sheet in the workbook has a tab at the bottom of the window. Initially the sheets are called Sheet1, Sheet2 etc. but these names can be changed to something more meaningful.

By default, Excel gives you three sheets for each workbook but this number can be increased when necessary – see page 100.

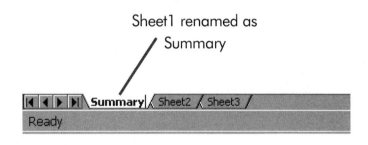

Sheet1 renamed as Summary

The View tab for Tools │ Options changes the way in which worksheets are displayed. Some of these features relate to the current worksheet only; others affect the whole workbook.

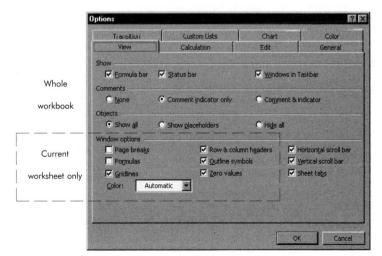

# Starting a new sheet

To start a new worksheet in the workbook, simply click on any of the sheet tabs at the bottom of the window: for example, Sheet2. You will be presented with a completely blank sheet, in which a new set of data, formulae and titles can be entered.

This sheet need have no connection with any other sheet in the workbook, other than the fact that all sheets are saved and loaded together.

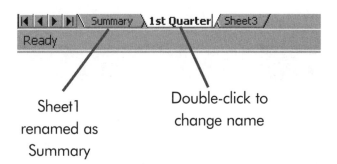

Sheet1 renamed as Summary

Double-click to change name

To start a new sheet:

1 Click on a new sheet tab to display a blank worksheet.

2 Double-click on the sheet tab to change the sheet name.

3 Start entering data and formulae, then save the workbook.

When you run out of blank sheets, you can insert a new one – see page 100. You can also change the order of the  sheets.

## Tip

If there are many sheets in the workbook, it may be worth putting a menu sheet at the front of the workbook with work-sheets selected by clicking on buttons – see page 143.

## Take note

If you make a major mistake in a sheet (for example, deleting the wrong range of cells), you should undo the error with [Ctrl]+[Z] immediately. Alternatively, close and re-open the file, restoring the file to the state it was in when you last saved it. Otherwise, if you move to another sheet, make changes and save the file, your mistakes in the first sheet will also be saved.

# Tab buttons

The four tab buttons work as follows:

☐ The first button displays the first sheet tab.

☐ The second button displays the previous tab on the left.

☐ The third button displays the next tab on the right.

☐ The fourth button displays the last sheet tab in the workbook.

You can switch from one sheet to another simply by clicking on the sheet tabs at the bottom of the window. When a tab is clicked, the corresponding sheet is displayed in the window and the sheet name is highlighted on the tab.

When you have a number of sheets, you will not be able to see all the tabs. The tabs can be scrolled to the left or right with the small tab buttons. Clicking on these buttons determines which tabs are displayed; it does not select a different sheet.

The bar along the bottom is shared by the sheet tabs and the horizontal scroll bars. You can change the amount used for each by dragging the divider to the left or right.

Show first tab    Show previous tab

Drag to change
share of bar

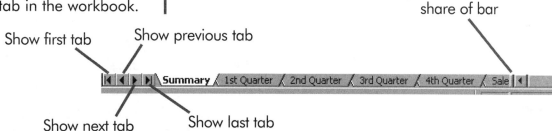

Show next tab    Show last tab

## Take note

When you select a different sheet, any changes you have made to the other sheets are not lost; the data is still held in memory. When you save the workbook, the contents of all sheets are saved.

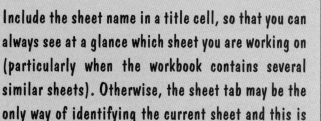

## Tip

Include the sheet name in a title cell, so that you can always see at a glance which sheet you are working on (particularly when the workbook contains several similar sheets). Otherwise, the sheet tab may be the only way of identifying the current sheet and this is not included when the file is printed.

# Multiple windows

You can display more than one worksheet from the file at a time by opening new windows onto the workbook. When you select the Window|New Window command, the effect is that a second window is opened, showing the same sheet.

The windows can be resized or moved to show data in the most convenient form, using the usual Windows actions (for an example of resized windows, see page 101). You may also need to change the scale of the display within the windows with the View|Zoom options.

These windows can be used independently. They show two different parts of the same worksheet or two different sheets from the workbook. You can enter data and formulae into either sheet. When you save the workbook, any changes made in either window are saved.

When you close the workbook (with File|Exit or by clicking on Close in the control menu) all subsidiary windows are closed. If any data has not been saved, you are given the opportunity to do so.

## Options

☐ You cannot view multiple windows if the worksheet window is maximised: click on the Maximize button to reduce the size.

☐ Use the Window|Arrange command to rearrange multiple windows.

Take note

If two windows show the same cells from a single sheet, any change in these cells in one window will be reflected in the display of the other window.

Tip

Although you can have several windows open at once, keep the number to a minimum. When there are too many windows, the screen becomes unnecessarily complicated.

Take note

You can also use File | Open to open a second workbook and display the worksheets from two different workbooks side by side.

## Basic steps

To mark a group of consecutive sheets:

1 Click on the first sheet tab.

2 Hold down the [Shift] key.

3 Click on the last sheet tab in the group.

To mark non-consecutive sheets:

1 Click on the first sheet tab.

2 Hold down the [Ctrl] key.

3 Click each of the other tabs in turn (clicking on the same tab a second time removes it from the group).

To cancel the selection, just click on a single tab without holding [Shift] or [Ctrl].

Sometimes you will want to work with more than one sheet at a time. For instance, you may want to put the same title in a series of sheets, or the row and column headings may be the same across all sheets.

A **group** of sheets can be selected: either a group of consecutive sheets or a selection of non-adjacent sheets. Any entry made in the current sheet will then be repeated in the corresponding cell in all other sheets in the group. (Any existing contents of those cells will be replaced.)

This gives you a quick way of filling a series of sheets. However, some care is needed when working on a group of sheets, as you may not be able to see all the sheets at once (depending on how you have arranged your windows).

## Take note

If you have entered the same value in several sheets, you can then edit any of the individual sheets without affecting the others (providing the group is no longer selected).

## Tip

If two or more sheets have similar entries, it is often quicker to enter the same value in all sheets and then edit some of them, than to enter each individually.

# Changing sheets

You are free to insert new sheets, copy sheets, change the order of sheets and delete unwanted sheets.

To insert a new sheet, click on one of the sheet tabs and then select Insert|Worksheet to add a new worksheet. The worksheet is inserted to the left of the selected sheet and becomes the active sheet. To add a new chart sheet, use Insert|Chart (see page 106 for details of charts).

You can add several worksheets at once by selecting the corresponding number of existing sheet tabs. For example, to insert three new sheets, first select a group of three existing tabs.

To delete an unwanted sheet, click on the sheet tab and then select Edit|Delete Sheet. (Always save the workbook first, in case you make a mistake – you cannot undo a worksheet deletion.)

## Insert options

New sheets are inserted as follows:

☐ By selecting the Insert| Worksheet command to add a new work-sheet or Insert | Chart to add a new chart.

☐ By clicking on the As New Sheet button in the final step when defining a chart (see page 111).

Charts on normal worksheets can also be converted to separate chart sheets (see page 116).

Take note

**The General tab for Tools |Options affects the over-all operation of Excel 2000. These options apply to all your work-books, not just the current one.**

---

**Options**  ? ✕

| Transition | Custom Lists | Chart | Color |
| View | Calculation | Edit | General |

Settings

☐ R1C1 reference style    ☐ Prompt for workbook properties
☐ Ignore other applications    ☐ Provide feedback with sound
    ☐ Zoom on roll with IntelliMouse

☑ Recently used file list: `4` entries    Web Options...

Sheets in new workbook: `3`

Standard font: `Arial`    Size: `10`

Default file location: `C:\excel data`

Alternate startup file location: ` `

User name: `Stephen Morris`

OK    Cancel

## Take note

The new order of sheets is only saved permanently when you save the workbook.

To move a sheet to a different position in the workbook, click on the sheet tab and then drag it across the tabs to its new position.

To make a copy of a sheet in the same workbook, click on the sheet tab, press and hold **[Ctrl]**, and then drag the tab to the point at which you want to insert the copy sheet.

You can move or copy a number of sheets if you start by marking a group of tabs.

The example below shows a workbook with two worksheets displayed. The sheets have been resized and repositioned.

First open window     Second open window

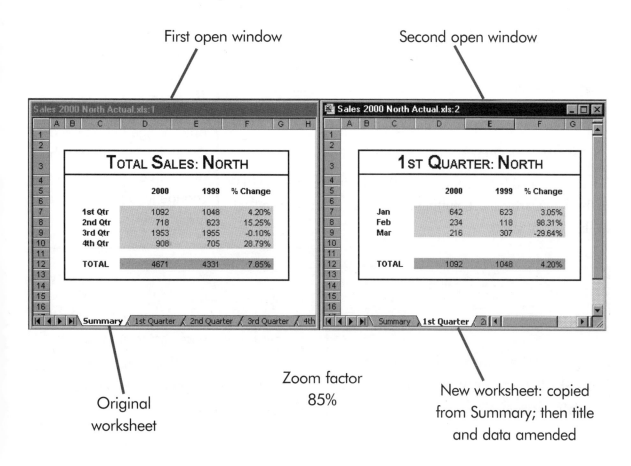

Zoom factor
85%

Original
worksheet

New worksheet: copied
from Summary; then title
and data amended

# Formulae across worksheets

A formula can refer to cells and ranges in other worksheets, or even a three-dimensional range covering several worksheets.

To reference a cell in another sheet, precede the cell reference with the sheet name and an exclamation mark. For instance, the summary sheet in the example will include the total value from cell D12 in the 1st Quarter worksheet if cell D7 contains the formula:

### ='1st Quarter'!D12

The single quotes are needed to avoid confusion, because of the space in the sheet name.

When this formula is copied to other cells, it is updated like any other relative reference (e.g. the value in E7 is '1st Quarter'!E12).

A formula may also refer to a range in another sheet:

### =SUM('1st Quarter'!D7:D9)

This formula adds the contents of all cells in the range D7:D9 in the 1st Quarter sheet, putting the answer in the selected cell of the current sheet.

To enter the total in D7 of the Summary sheet:

1 Display two windows for the workbook, one showing the Summary sheet, the other the 1st Quarter sheet.

2 Click on D7 in the Summary sheet.

3 Type = in the cell.

4 Click on the 1st Quarter sheet and then on cell D12; the formula is updated as you do so.

5 Press [Enter].

Any change in D7, D8 or D9 in the 1st Quarter sheet results in a corresponding change in D7 in the Summary sheet.

## Take note

If you insert or delete rows and columns in one sheet, the formulae in other sheets are updated accordingly.

## Tip

If you need to use quotes in sheet references use ordinary single quotes. Don't try to insert 'smart quotes'; Excel will not recognise these.

**Take note**

You can open more than one workbook at a time and transfer data between any of the windows using the standard cut, copy and paste options.

**Take note**

If you insert or delete sheets, or move any sheet referred to in the 3-D reference, the results of any affected formulae will be updated.

A formula can refer to a three-dimensional block of cells that covers two or more consecutive sheets. The range of sheets is placed before the exclamation mark, the range of cells after it.

For example, the grand total of sales in the Summary sheet could just as well have been calculated by:

**=SUM('1st Quarter:4th Quarter'!D7:D9)**

This will add the contents of all cells in the range D7:D9 in all sheets from 1st Quarter to 4th Quarter. In three-dimensional references, the same range of cells is used in all sheets. If you think of the sheets as lying one above another, this effectively gives you a three-dimensional rectangular block of cells.

If a sheet name uses characters other than numbers and letters (e.g. 1st Quarter), any sheet reference must be enclosed in single quotes. The quotes are not needed for single-word names that contain only numbers and letters (e.g. Summary, Sheet1). For ranges of sheets, a single pair of quotes encloses both sheet names (as in '1st Quarter:4th Quarter'). Only use straight quotes, as typed on the keyboard, not 'smart quotes'.

You can also link to cells in another workbook. Open two workbooks and create the formula in the same way as for linking across two worksheets. The formula will include the workbook name in square brackets; for example:

**='[Area51.xls]Totals'!$E$9**

This is an absolute reference to cell E9 on the Totals sheet of the workbook in Area51.xls.

When you load a file with formulae that refer to other workbooks, you are given the opportunity to update the current values.

# Summary

- ❑  An Excel file is called a **workbook** and may contain many separate sheets.

- ❑  Each sheet is a worksheet or chart sheet.

- ❑  To start a new sheet, click on a sheet tab.

- ❑  Use the tab buttons to display further sheet tabs.

- ❑  Open additional windows on the sheet with Window|New Window.

- ❑  Open other files with File | Open.

- ❑  Use Window | Arrange to display multiple sheets simultaneously.

- ❑  Sheets can be inserted, deleted, copied and moved.

- ❑  Formulae can refer to ranges on other sheets or three-dimensional ranges covering several sheets.

- ❑  Formulae can also link to cells or ranges in other files.

# 12 Charts and graphics

# Chart Wizard

Excel 2000 provides a wide range of options for displaying any set of data as a chart or graph: bar charts, pie charts, line graphs and others. The chart can be placed anywhere on the worksheet and can be made to fit a rectangle of any size or shape. Once it has been created, any aspects of the chart can be changed. Alternatively, you can create a separate chart sheet.

A chart is created on a worksheet using the Chart Wizard, which provides you with a series of dialog boxes that are used to build up the chart.

Before starting Chart Wizard, you should mark the block of data to be charted.

## Basic steps

1  Mark the range of data for which the chart is to be created. Include the row of labels above the data and the column to the left, if appropriate.

2  Click on the Chart Wizard button. The first of four dialog boxes is displayed.

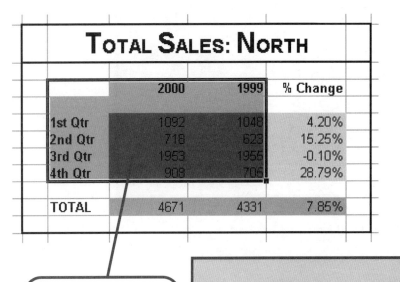

1  Mark data area

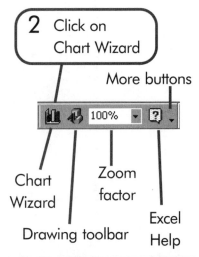

2  Click on Chart Wizard

More buttons

Chart Wizard

Zoom factor

Drawing toolbar

Excel Help

## Take note

You can include blank rows and columns in the range – these will be ignored. The range can be made up of non-adjacent blocks, if the data comes from different parts of the sheet.

3 Click on a chart type. The default is the Column chart but there are 13 other types. The dialog box shows several variations of the selected type.

4 Click on a sub-type and then on Next.

Chart Wizard offers 14 different types of chart. These fall into three broad categories:

- Bar charts have a rectangular bar for each item of data, the height of the bar being proportional to the data value.

- Graphs plot a series of points, with each point being determined by a pair of co-ordinates. Usually, consecutive points are joined together by a line.

- Pie charts consist of a circle divided into segments. The values in the data series are totalled, so that each value can be calculated as a percentage of the total. The sizes of the segments are proportional to these percentages.

The options provided are variations on these: for instance, three-dimensional bars or area graphs (where the value is represented by the area under the graph).

Take note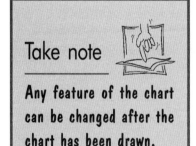

Any feature of the chart can be changed after the chart has been drawn.

4 Click on a sub-type

3 Click on a chart type

Take note

The Custom Types tab has additional, more interesting variations.

The data range consists of one or more rows or columns; each row or column will provide the data for one series of bars or for one line on a line graph.

You can choose either rows or columns for the data series. If you choose rows, the data values in each row form one set of bars or the points on one line; the column headings are the labels for the chart. If you choose columns, each column is a data series and the row headings are used as chart labels.

*By columns: quarters on the X-axis; set of bars for each year*

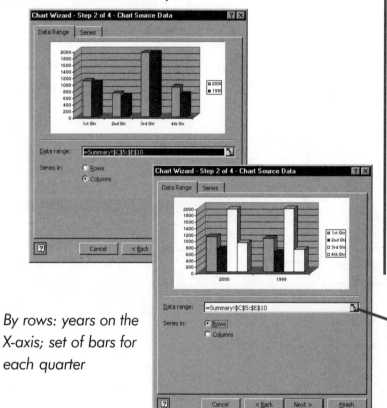

*By rows: years on the X-axis; set of bars for each quarter*

5   The second dialog box gives you the opportunity to change the data range that has been selected. You either mark the range by dragging the pointer on the worksheet or edit the range in the dialog box.

To mark a new range, click on the icon on the right of the Data Range. The Chart Wizard is reduced to a small box. Mark the data area (including labels), then click on the icon on the right of the reduced dialog box.

6   Select either rows or columns as the basis for the data series.

Click to change range

Click after marking range

Chart Wizard - Step 2 of 4 - Chart Source Data - Data range:
=Summary!$C$5:$E$10

**7** Click on the Series tab and change the ranges that identify the series names, values and X-axis labels. Click on Next when the ranges are correct.

Within the data range, you should have a block of data and the labels that will be shown on the graph. The Series tab for Step 2 lets you change these ranges.

There will be one graph or one set of bars for each series. For each of these series you can identify a range containing the series name (e.g. the year) and a range of values.

The range for the X-axis labels defines the cells whose contents will be printed along the bottom of the chart.

You can mark any range by clicking on the icon to the right of the entry box.

Take note

**At any step, clicking on Back takes you back to the previous step, where you can make further changes.**

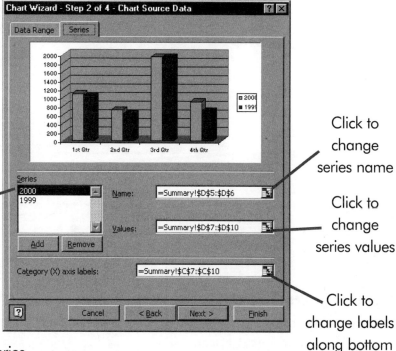

Select series

Click to change series name

Click to change series values

Click to change labels along bottom of chart

Current settings for '2000' series
Series name (D5:D6)          2000
Values (D7:D10)              1092 to 908
Category labels (C7:C10)     1st Qtr to 4th Qtr

The third dialog box lets you add explanatory text to the chart. The **chart title** is printed above the graph, and the **axis titles** are added alongside the axis labels. Other tabs let you alter other features of the chart. For example, the **legend** is a box showing the colours or types of points used for each data series.

8 Enter some text for the chart title and for each of the axes. Make any further changes with the other tabs, then click on Next.

Chart title

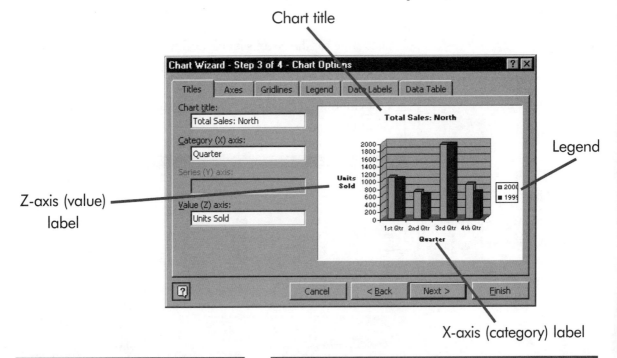

Legend

Z-axis (value) label

X-axis (category) label

## Tip

Keep the titles simple and avoid cluttering the borders of the graph with too much text. If you want to add extra notes, you can use a text box - see page 120.

## Take note

You can edit the text of the titles later and apply different fonts if required. The legend box can also be switched on or off, and moved to a different position; any of the other chart features can be changed (see page 112).

**9** Choose the location for the chart: a separate sheet or an existing worksheet.

Click on Finish. The new chart will be displayed and can be edited if necessary.

The final dialog box gives you the choice between overlaying the new chart on one of the worksheets (As Object In) or placing it in a new sheet (As New Sheet).

If you choose to keep the chart on an existing worksheet, you can select a different sheet from the drop-down list.

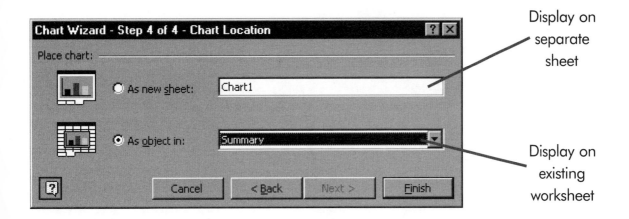

Display on separate sheet

Display on existing worksheet

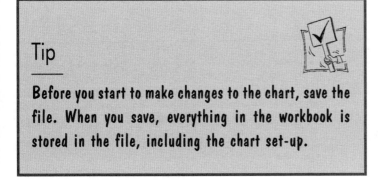

## Tip

Before you start to make changes to the chart, save the file. When you save, everything in the workbook is stored in the file, including the chart set-up.

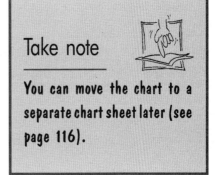

## Take note

You can move the chart to a separate chart sheet later (see page 116).

# Editing the chart

When the chart has been drawn, it can be moved to a new position on the sheet and can be resized to fit any reasonable gap.

If you place the mouse pointer over any part of the chart, a descriptive label pops up. If you point to a data item, the label shows you the series name and data value.

☐ To move the chart, click on it and then drag it to a new position.

☐ To change the size, click on the chart and then drag the sizing handles on the corners and sides. Hold down the [Shift] key while you drag to keep the proportions the same.

☐ To remove a chart from a sheet, click on the chart and press [Delete].

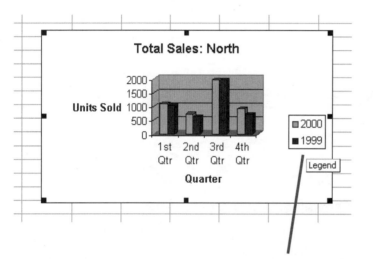

Point to a bar to display series name and data value

Point to a chart feature to display a description

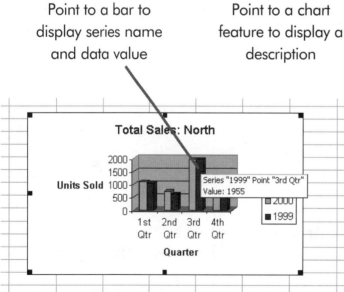

## Take note

The chart is laid over the top of the sheet. It does not affect any data on the underlying sheet and formulae still act in the same way, even if the data or formula cells are hidden by the chart.

# Basic steps

To edit any feature of the chart:

1 Double-click on any item on the chart: text, labels, grid lines, grid background, legend, bars or lines, etc.

2 In the dialog box that appears, make any changes that are needed to the appearance of the chart.

The chart produced so far was selected from only a limited number of options. You are now free to change any aspect of the chart: colours, fonts, patterns, line styles and so on.

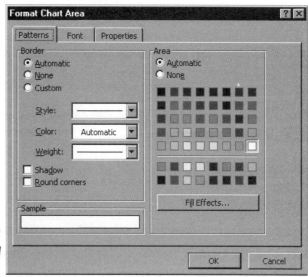

*Options for chart area (chart background, font and general properties)*

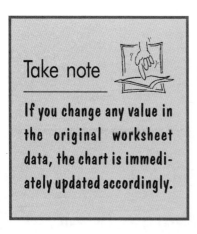

## Take note

**If you change any value in the original worksheet data, the chart is immediately updated accordingly.**

*Options for axes*

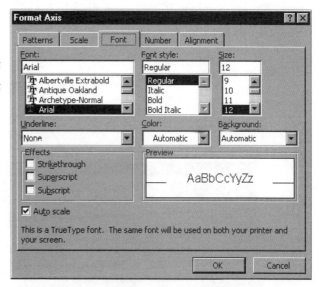

The Chart toolbar provides options for making quick changes to certain aspects of the chart.

# Changing chart data

You can change the range of data displayed on the chart at any time.

- New rows or columns can be added, increasing the scope of the chart.

- The range can be extended or contracted to show more or less data.

- The range can be changed completely, so that it covers a different set of data.

- Data series can be removed from the chart.

All of these tasks can be accomplished by clicking on the chart and then selecting the Chart | Source Data option and the Series tab. You can change the ranges for any of the series or click on Add to add a new series, Remove to delete a series from the chart. There are also alternative methods for making some of these changes.

Choose new series or extra points for existing series

Select direction of data series

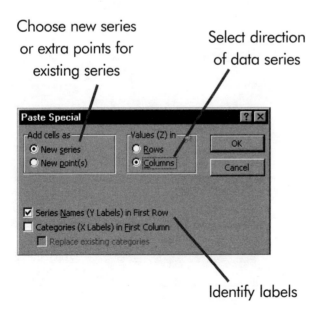

Identify labels

## Alternatives

To add a new data series or extend an existing series:

1 Mark the new range (including labels).

2 Click on the range border and drag it into the chart.

3 Unless it is obvious to Excel how the data is to be displayed, you will be asked to fill in a dialog box (see below).

4 The chart is extended to show the new data.

To delete a data series from the chart:

1 Click on one of the bars or data points.

2 Press [Delete].

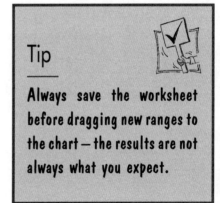

Tip

**Always save the worksheet before dragging new ranges to the chart — the results are not always what you expect.**

To change the view for a
3-D chart:

1  Click on the chart to
select it.

2  Select 3-D View from
the Chart menu.

3  To rotate the chart
horizontally, click on
one of the buttons
below the chart.

4  To rotate the chart
vertically, click on the
buttons to the left of the
chart.

5  Click on Apply to see
the effect of the current
settings and OK to
finish.

When a chart has been selected by double-clicking on it, some
of the menus at the top of the window change. For instance, the
options are reduced in the Insert and View menus; the Format
menu provides a new range of options for changing the way in
which the chart is displayed.

There is also a new Chart menu, replacing the Data menu. The
first four options in the expanded menu correspond to the four
steps in the Chart Wizard, and bring up the same dialog boxes.

The Chart|Add Trendline option performs regression analysis
on a bar chart or graph, allowing you to predict future values by
extending the trend line beyond the actual data.

The Chart | 3-D View option allows you to rotate a three-
dimensional chart, both horizontally and vertically.

Rotate
vertically

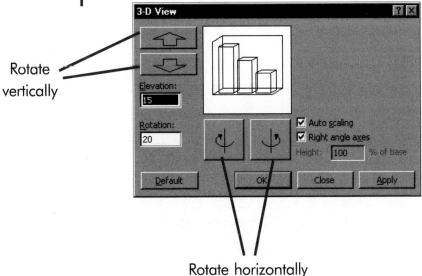

Rotate horizontally

# Chart sheets

Much of the time you will include charts as part of a normal worksheet. However, you may want to use a chart as a transparency for an overhead projector, as a handout during a presentation, or simply as an individual page in a report. In these cases, you can create a separate **chart sheet** within the workbook.

The chart sheet can be created from scratch or derived from an existing chart on a worksheet.

Click to convert to chart sheet

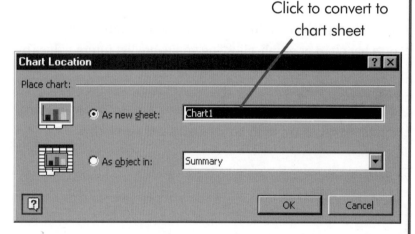

To create a new chart sheet:

1 Mark the range to be charted.

2 Select Chart from the Insert menu and then select As New Sheet.

3 Complete the Chart Wizard dialog boxes, as before.

The result is that a new sheet is created (this time, a chart sheet), with a default name of Chart1.

To convert an existing worksheet into a chart sheet:

1 Click on the chart.

2 Select Location from the Chart menu.

3 Click on As New Sheet in the Chart Location dialog box.

4 Click on OK.

The new sheet is created and can be renamed.

## Tip

You can create a chart sheet quickly by marking a range and then pressing [F11]. The chart thst is created uses all the default settings.

## Take note

The View | Full Screen option expands a chart (or a worksheet) so that it fills the whole screen, with only the menu bar and sheet tabs showing.

# Options

☐ Rename the sheet by double-clicking on the sheet tab.

☐ Change the position of the sheet in the workbook by dragging the sheet tab to a new position.

☐ Delete the chart sheet by selecting it and then choosing Delete Sheet from the Edit menu.

The chart shcet behaves in the same way as a worksheet and is saved as part of the workbook. The chart sheet can be renamed, moved to a new position or deleted. You can also display it in a separate window or print it.

*Chart sheet shown at Full Screen*

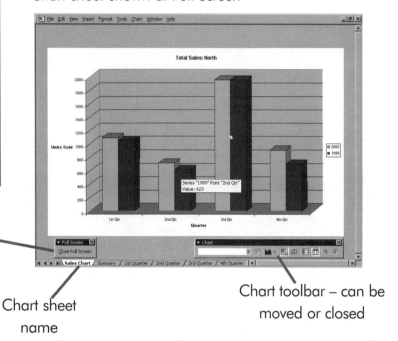

Full Screen toolbar – click button for normal view

Chart sheet name

Chart toolbar – can be moved or closed

---

## Take note

You can copy a chart from a worksheet to a chart sheet. Click once on the chart (so that the sizing handles are shown at the corners) and press [Ctrl]+[C] to copy it to the Clipboard; then open the chart sheet and press [Ctrl]+[V] to paste in the chart.

Similarly, you can copy a chart from a chart sheet onto a worksheet. In this case you must click in the area outside the chart, so that the sizing handles are shown on the corners of the chart sheet.

# Graphic objects

Excel allows you to add lines, shapes and text to the worksheet. These objects are laid over the top of the sheet, in the same way as charts. Therefore they do not affect the data and formulae below.

Each object is a separate entity and can be manipulated independently of any other object. The objects are selected from the Drawing toolbar.

To add an object:

1 Click on the Drawing button. The toolbar is displayed.

2 Click on any shape or line on the toolbar and then mark it out on the worksheet.

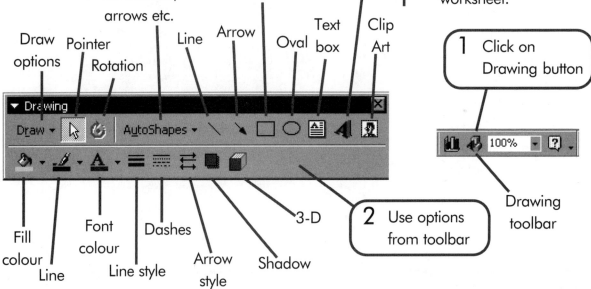

Connectors, arrows etc.

Rectangle    WordArt

Draw options    Pointer    Rotation    Line    Arrow    Oval    Text box    Clip Art

Fill colour    Font colour    Dashes    3-D

Line colour    Line style    Arrow style    Shadow

1 Click on Drawing button

2 Use options from toolbar

Drawing toolbar

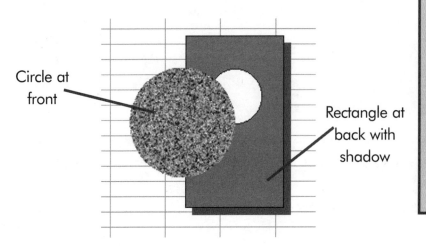

Circle at front

Rectangle at back with shadow

## Tip

To draw a perfect circle or square, select the ellipse or rectangle and then hold down the [Shift] key while you mark out the shape.

# Options

- To move an object, click on it and then drag it to a new position.

- To delete an object, click on it and then press [Delete].

**Tip**
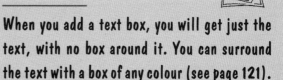

The arrow and text box are particularly useful for adding comments to charts.

**Take note**

Like all Excel toolbars, the Drawing toolbar can be dragged from its default position above the status bar onto the sheet itself. It can also be resized.

Graphic objects can be moved, resized and deleted. You can also change the colour or background pattern for an object by selecting from the palette on the Drawing toolbox.

Two or more objects can be grouped together by holding down the **[Shift]** key and clicking on them, then clicking on Group in the Draw options (a drop-down menu on the left of the Drawing toolbar, which includes Group in its hidden options). When objects are in a group, they are treated as a single object for the purposes of moving them, changing the colour and pattern, and so on. To make the objects independent again, click on an object in the group and then on Ungroup in the Draw options.

**Take note**

When you add a text box, you will get just the text, with no box around it. You can surround the text with a box of any colour (see page 121).

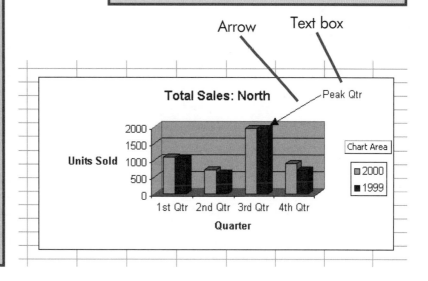

119

# Text boxes

Although you can add text to a worksheet by typing into a cell, there are occasions when it is useful to have a more flexible approach. The use of text boxes lets you add any piece of text to the worksheet, at any position.

For example, you can add a heading as a text box, and apply to it any font and box format you like.

Since these boxes are independent of the main sheet, there is no effect on the underlying sheet. Therefore, you can have large headings or small annotations without the need to change the row heights to fit the text. This is useful if you want to add text to the side of other data, using a different point size.

## Basic steps

To add a text box:

1 Click on the Text Box button in the Drawing toolbar.

2 Mark the area to be covered by the text box.

3 Enter the text.

**Tip**

Text boxes are also useful for annotating charts; you can add any piece of text at any point on a chart.

Text box

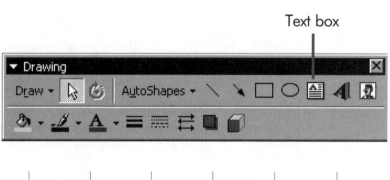

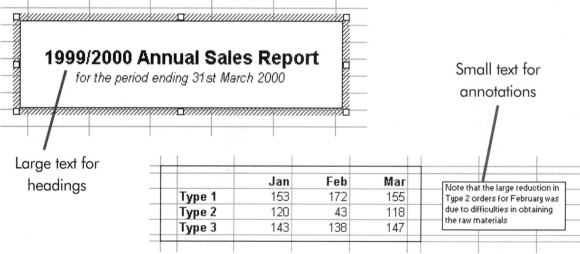

Large text for headings

Small text for annotations

1999/2000 Annual Sales Report
for the period ending 31st March 2000

Note that the large reduction in Type 2 orders for February was due to difficulties in obtaining the raw materials

|        | Jan | Feb | Mar |
|--------|-----|-----|-----|
| Type 1 | 153 | 172 | 155 |
| Type 2 | 120 | 43  | 118 |
| Type 3 | 143 | 138 | 147 |

The text box and its contents can be edited in a variety of ways:

● Click on the box to select it. (It is given a shaded border.) You can then apply a pattern or colour to the box around the text.

● Drag the sides of the box to move it or the sizing handles to change its size.

● Click on the box again to edit the text. Any part of the text can be marked and have its typeface, size, attributes and colour changed, in the same way as for text in a cell.

● The text can be left-aligned, centred or right-aligned.

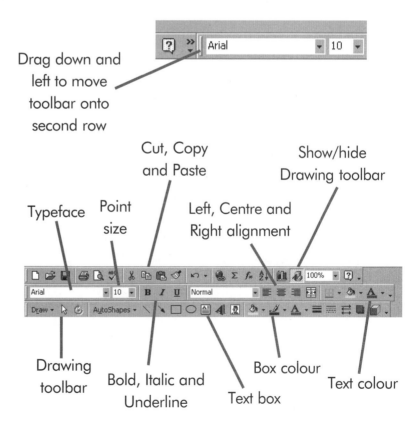

# Summary

❑ Any blocks of data can be represented by a chart or graph.

❑ Charts and graphs may be embedded on the worksheet or on separate chart sheets in the workbook.

❑ The Chart Wizard is a set of four dialog boxes that determine the chart type and any text attached to it.

❑ Charts can be moved or resized; they do not affect the underlying data and formulae.

❑ Any change to the data results in a corresponding change to the chart.

❑ Graphic objects are added with the Drawing toolbar.

❑ Text boxes can be overlaid on any part of a worksheet or chart. Any typeface, size, attributes or colour can be used for any part of the text, without affecting the worksheet below.

# 13 Printing

# Printer set-up

Traditionally, printing has always been the most fraught and unpredictable part of any computer process – and there is little point in going to the trouble of entering information on the computer if you cannot produce printed output. Fortunately, printing is one aspect of computer use that has become much easier with the advent of Windows. If you can produce output from one Windows application, then you should be able to do so from any other.

The first stage is to check that Windows is set up correctly for printing.

1 Select Settings in the Windows Start menu and click on Printers. The Printers folder is opened.

2 Double-click on the icon for your most frequently-used printer.

3 Click on Set As Default in the Printer menu to set the printer as the Windows default.

4 Click on Properties in the Printer menu to change other default features (orientation, margins, scaling etc.)

Printers folder (lists printers that have been installed on your computer)

Double-click to set up printer

Click here to set printer as default

Further set-up options

# Further options

- The General box allows you to enter comments, print an information page at the start of each print run (useful for net-worked printers) and print a test page.

- The Details box selects the printer port, printer driver and other hardware infor-mation.

- The Paper box lets you choose the paper tray (for printers with more than one), size of paper, orientation (which way round the paper is to be printed) and default number of copies.

- The Graphics box sets resolution and scaling.

- The remaining tabs set fonts, memory, printer instructions and other details.

The Properties option in the Printer menu leads to a box of set-up information. This has two or more tabs, each of which sets a number of printer options. All of these set defaults that are applied each time you print but can be overridden on any particular print run.

The options that are provided vary, depending on the type of printer that has been selected.

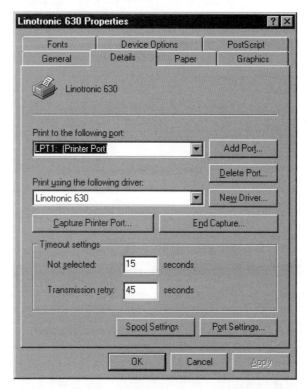

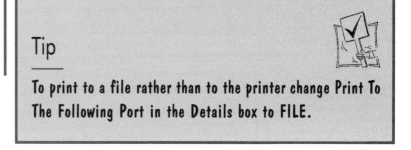

## Tip

To print to a file rather than to the printer change Print To The Following Port in the Details box to FILE.

# Page set-up

The Page Setup option in the Excel 2000 File menu lets you determine the way in which a particular sheet will be printed. There are four tabs, the first of which contains the Page settings:

- **Orientation** gives you either portrait (tall, thin) pages or landscape (pages printed sideways).

- **Scaling** is either a fixed percentage (e.g. 50% to reduce everything to half size) or the largest size possible for the sheets to fit the page. For best-fit scaling, choose the number of pages to be printed.

- **Paper size** provides a range of standard page sizes.

- **Print quality** is available only for some types of printer (e.g. draft and letter quality for some dot matrix printers).

- **First page number** determines the page number for the first page: AUTO defaults to 1, unless this print run follows on from another, in which case page numbering carries on from the previous run.

1 In Excel, select Page Setup from the File menu.

2 Click on the Page tab (if necessary).

3 Select the required options.

## Page Setup dialog

Page Setup

| Page | Margins | Header/Footer | Sheet |

Orientation

A  ⦿ Portrait    A  ○ Landscape

Print...
Print Preview
Options...

Scaling

⦿ Adjust to: [100] % normal size
○ Fit to: [1] page(s) wide by [1] tall

Paper size: [A4]
Print quality: [300 dpi]
First page number: [Auto]

OK    Cancel

**Tip**

On page printers, there is a certain margin on each edge where nothing can be printed. Make sure your margin settings are large enough to include this area.

# Options

# Margins

- ☐ The Top margin is the space above the main text area, including the space used by the header.

- ☐ The Bottom margin is the space below the text area, including any footer.

- ☐ The Left and Right margins are the spaces on either side.

- ☐ The Header and Footer settings determine the positions of the header and footer within the top and bottom margins (being the distance from the edge of the paper).

- ☐ The Center on Page options let you centre any sheet that does not fill the page. The sheet can be centred horizontally, vertically or both.

The Margins tab on the Page Setup box lets you decide how much blank space there should be at the top, bottom and sides of the sheet.

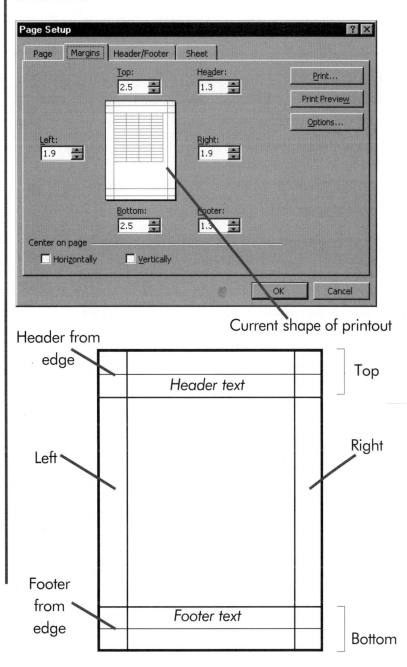

# Headers and footers

You can choose a piece of text to be printed at the top and bottom of every page. The header and footer can cover several lines and each has three sections: for printing on the left, right or centre of the page.

A standard header/footer can be selected from the list, which offers defaults such as the sheet name, the filename, your name or your company name, and various combinations. Alternatively, you can create your own headers and footers by clicking on the Custom buttons. Each header/footer can contain any text (which can be formatted in the usual way) plus a variety of special codes: page number, total pages, current date, time, filename and worksheet name.

☐ The Header is a piece of text that is printed at the top of each page.

☐ The Footer is text that appears at the bottom of every page.

| | |
|---|---|
| # | Page number |
| 🗒 | Total pages |
| 🗓 | Current date |
| 🕐 | Current time |
| 📄 | Filename |
| 🖹 | Worksheet tab name |

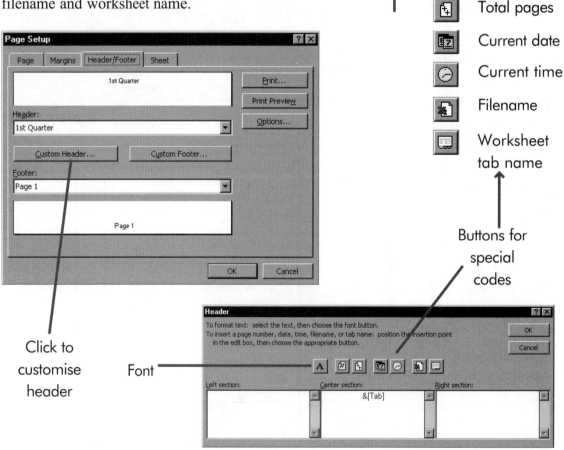

Click to customise header

Font

Buttons for special codes

128

# Options

☐ The Print Area is the default range to be printed.

☐ The Print Titles are rows and columns that are to be repeated on every page when the worksheet will not fit on one page.

☐ The Print options decide which optional features will be printed.

☐ The Page Order is used when the worksheet is both too long and too wide for one page; it decides whether printing is done from top to bottom and then left to right, or vice versa.

# Sheet settings

The final Page Setup tab determines the way in which the sheet itself is printed.

You can select the ranges for the Print Area and Print Titles by clicking on the icons on the right of the text boxes.

Click to select a range

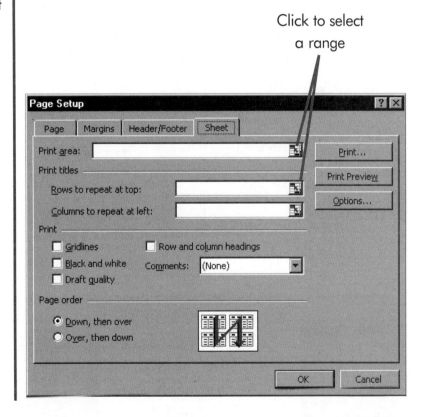

Tip

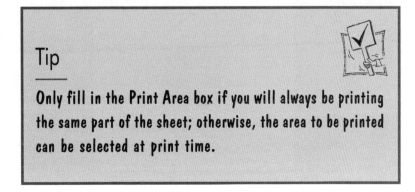

Only fill in the Print Area box if you will always be printing the same part of the sheet; otherwise, the area to be printed can be selected at print time.

# Preview

The Print Preview option in the File menu lets you see on screen what the final printed page will look like. As well as zooming into or out of the display, there are options to take you directly to other printer activities (as a shortcut to the File menu).

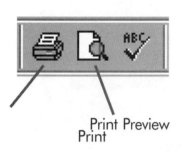

Print Preview
Print

Page as it will appear when printed

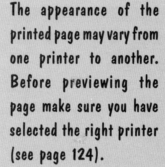

## Take note

The appearance of the printed page may vary from one printer to another. Before previewing the page make sure you have selected the right printer (see page 124).

## Options

Next displays the next page.

Previous displays the previous page.

Zoom expands or contracts the display.

Print takes you to the File | Print options.

Setup loads Page Setup.

Margins lets you change the page margins.

Page Break Preview lets you see the page breaks and change them.

Close returns you to the worksheet.

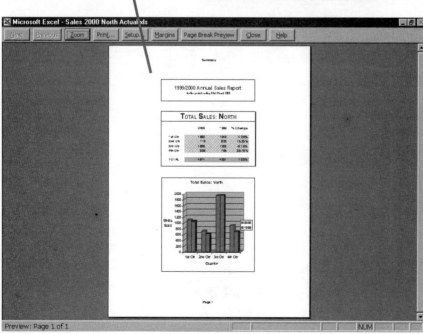

The information to be printed is chosen (in the Print What box) from:

☐ Selection: the part of the worksheet previously marked by dragging the pointer over a range

☐ Active Sheet(s): those sheets whose tabs are currently selected

☐ Entire Workbook: all sheets

You can limit the amount printed by selecting a range of pages, rather than All.

You can also specify the number of copies to print.

Once all the set-up work has been completed (and this is something you should only have to do once for each workbook), you can start printing. The File | Print command has a very simple dialog box although, in common with the other print commands, it has buttons to take you to other set-up stages.

Printer properties

**Print**

Printer
Name: Linotronic 630    Properties
Status: Idle
Type: Linotronic 630
Where: LPT1:
Comment:                    ☐ Print to file

Print range
⦿ All
○ Page(s) From: ▢ To: ▢

Print what
○ Selection    ○ Entire workbook
⦿ Active sheet(s)

Copies
Number of copies: ▢

 ☑ Collate

Preview    OK    Cancel

Page preview

## Tip

You will not always want to print the whole sheet, so leave the Print Area blank in the Sheet settings and just mark a suitable range each time before you print. Remember that you can mark whole rows or columns by clicking on the row numbers or column letters. When you are ready to print the whole sheet, click on the empty box in the top left-hand corner of the sheet.

# Summary

- ❑ Printing is controlled by Windows and its Printers folder.

- ❑ The Excel 2000 Page Setup lets you decide details of page layout, margins, headers and footers, and area to be printed.

- ❑ Headers are lines of text printed at the top of each page; footers are printed at the bottom of the page.

- ❑ Headers and footers can include special codes for page number, total pages, current date and time, filename and worksheet name.

- ❑ Print Preview allows you to see on screen what the page will look like when printed.

- ❑ You can print the entire workbook, a selection of sheets or just the range that is currently selected.

# 14 Advanced features

# Sorting data

The basic principles for using Excel 2000 have now been covered. However, Excel contains many more facilities, some extremely useful, others rather obscure. This chapter looks briefly at a few of the additional features on offer.

Sorting data is one of the easiest tasks and has many uses. Simple sorting involves marking a range and then clicking on one of the sort buttons, to sort the contents of the cells in either ascending (A to Z) or descending (Z to A) order.

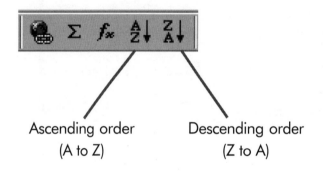

Ascending order
(A to Z)

Descending order
(Z to A)

## Rules

- ☐ All numeric values come before text values and are sorted in order of magnitude.

- ☐ Numbers entered as text are sorted character by character (so '12' is before '3', because the character '1' comes before '3').

- ☐ Characters other than numbers and letters are first in the sort order, followed by numeric characters and then alphabetic letters.

- ☐ Upper and lower case letters are treated the same, unless you specify otherwise.

Unsorted

| Albert |  | -623 |  |
|---|---|---|---|
| (also) |  | 0.999 |  |
| --- ends --- |  | 3.14159 |  |
| aardvark |  | 78 |  |
| 125 train |  | 128 |  |
| {yes} |  | --- ends --- |  |
| A |  | (also) |  |
| Beethoven |  | {yes} |  |
| 33 rpm |  | 125 train |  |
| beetroot |  | 33 rpm |  |
| 128 |  | A |  |
| 78 |  | aardvark |  |
| 3.14159 |  | Albert |  |
| -623 |  | Beethoven |  |
| 0.999 |  | beetroot |  |

Sorted

# Basic steps

1 Select Sort from the Data menu.

2 Choose the columns on which the sort is to be based (selecting from the list of currently highlighted columns).

3 For each sort column, choose Ascending or Descending order.

4 Specify whether or not there is a header row. (The header row will not be included in the sort.)

5 Click on the Options button to further refine the sort. Click on OK to close the Sort Options dialog box.

6 Click on OK to perform the sort.

For a more sophisticated sort, select Sort from the Data menu. This allows you to choose up to three columns for sorting. If the entries in the first sort column are the same, the sort is based on the second column; if these are also identical, the order is determined by the third column.

You can choose ascending or descending order for each column independently, and also make the sort case-sensitive (with capitals before lower-case letters).

1 Select Sort | Data

3 Choose sort direction

2 Choose sort columns

4 Header row

5 Refine the sort

6 Start the sort

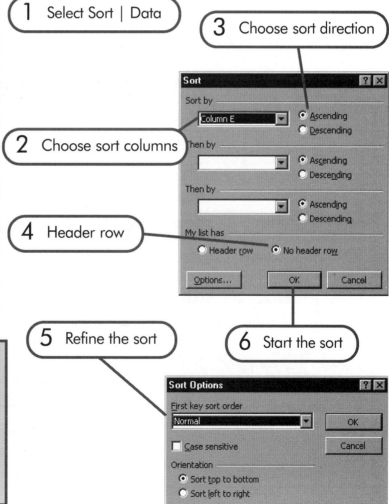

## Tip

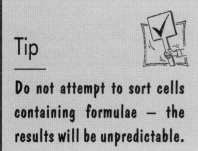

**Do not attempt to sort cells containing formulae — the results will be unpredictable.**

# Find and replace

The Find option in the Edit Menu searches the worksheet for a specified piece of text. This may be a word, a phrase or just a few characters from a word. The search will be in formulae and values, unless you specify **Values** (in which case formulae are ignored). The search is in the whole worksheet, unless you have marked a range or selected a group of worksheets.

The Replace option searches for one piece of text and then replaces it with another one.

Text to find

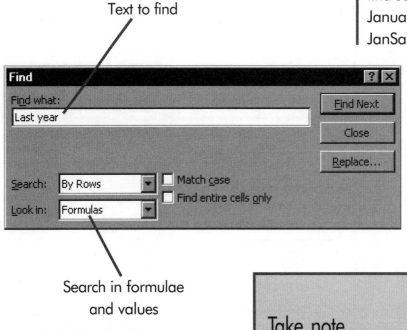

Search in formulae
and values

Spelling checker

## Wildcards

Two wildcards can be used in the Find command:

☐ ? represents any single character.

☐ * represents any group of characters (or no characters).

For example, Jan*Sales will find Jan 2000 Sales , January Sales and JanSales.

## Take note

The Spelling option from the Tools menu will check all text in the worksheet against its built-in dictionary and warn you of any words it does not recognise, with suggested replacements.

136

# Basic steps

# Toolbars

To create a new toolbar:

1 Select View | Toolbars.

2 Click on Customize.

3 Click on the New button. Enter a name for the toolbar and click on OK.

4 Click on the Commands tab.

5 Select a Category.

6 Drag an icon to the new toolbar (which will be 'floating' somewhere nearby).

Repeat steps 5 and 6 until the toolbar is complete, then click on Close.

Excel is equipped with a number of toolbars, which can be customised to suit your own preferences. The View | Toolbars command lists the toolbars. Clicking on the boxes next to the toolbar names displays or hides the toolbars.

To change the contents of the toolbars, click on Customize:

● New buttons are added to the toolbars by dragging the buttons from the Commands tab of the dialog box to the toolbars.

● Buttons are removed from toolbars by dragging them off the toolbars.

● Clicking on the New button creates a new toolbar.

Defaults

Available toolbars

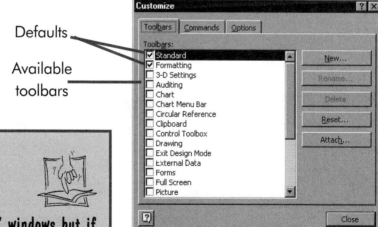

## Take note

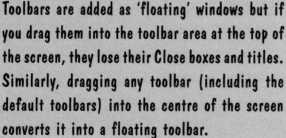

Toolbars are added as 'floating' windows but if you drag them into the toolbar area at the top of the screen, they lose their Close boxes and titles. Similarly, dragging any toolbar (including the default toolbars) into the centre of the screen converts it into a floating toolbar.

*Custom toolbar*

137

# Comments

Data can be annotated by attaching a comment to any cell. The comment takes the form of a piece of text entered into a dialog box using Insert | Comment. All the usual editing facilities are available. Comments are saved with the worksheet.

The comment attached to a cell is displayed if you pause with the pointer over the cell. All comments for the worksheet can be viewed with View | Comments and any comment can be edited or deleted.

The Comments toolbar provides viewing and editing facilities.

To add a comment:

1 Click on a cell.

2 Select Insert | Comment.

3 Type the text into the comment box.

4 Click on a different cell.

A red triangle in the top right-hand corner of the cell indicates that a comment is attached.

Cell to which comment is attached

Enter text of comment here (user name given as default)

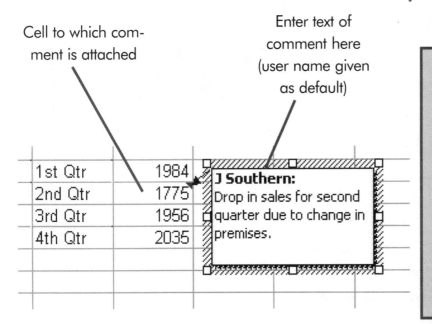

| 1st Qtr | 1984 |
| 2nd Qtr | 1775 |
| 3rd Qtr | 1956 |
| 4th Qtr | 2035 |

**J Southern:**
Drop in sales for second quarter due to change in premises.

## Tip

**To provide easy access to comments, add the New Comment button to one of the toolbars. This button can be found in the Insert category and is a shortcut to Insert | Comment.**

*Comments toolbar*

New Comment button

## Basic steps

1 Select Insert | Picture | From File.

2 Open the folder containing the picture file.

3 Click on the filename.

4 Click on OK.

Bitmaps, Windows metafiles and other pictures can be added to the Excel worksheets, as illustrations or to enhance the appearance of the finished sheet. For example, you could create a company logo in Paint and then add this to the top of all your reports.

Pictures are added with the Insert | Picture menu. In the same way as text boxes, charts and graphic objects, pictures are overlaid on the sheet and have no effect on the underlying data and formulae.

The pictures can be moved by dragging them or resized by dragging their sizing handles. Other formatting options are available by selecting Format | Picture.

List of picture files in selected folder

Picture file currently highlighted

Change file type to restrict list or show all files

Enter filename with wildcards to restrict list (e.g. b*.bmp)

Click to insert highlighted picture

# Macros

A **macro** is a way of automating a series of frequently-needed actions. At its simplest, a macro is created by recording a series of actions which are then replayed.

Valid Excel name

Store macro in current workbook, a new workbook or your Personal Macro Workbook (making the macro available to all your workbooks)

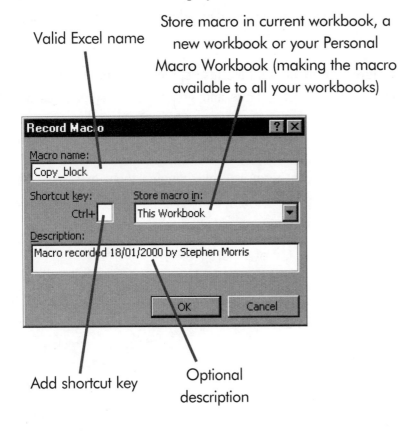

Add shortcut key

Optional description

To record a macro:

1 Select Tools | Macro and click on Record New Macro.

2 Enter a name for the macro and description. The name must be a valid Excel name (letters, numbers, underscore; no spaces).

3 If required, type a letter to be used with [Ctrl] as a shortcut to the macro.

4 Click on OK.

5 Any actions you now take are recorded, including any mistakes you make!

6 When you have finished, click on the Stop button.

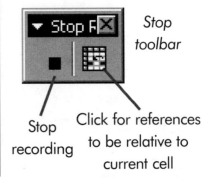

Stop toolbar

Stop recording

Click for references to be relative to current cell

## Take note

By default, all cell references are absolute; i.e. the same cells will be used regardless of which cell is current when the macro is run. For the macro to perform its actions relative to the start position, click on the Relative Reference button.

# Buttons

The Macro box has the following buttons:

☐ Run runs the macro.

☐ Cancel returns you to the worksheet.

☐ Step Into runs the macro one step at a time, so you can see how it works and detect bugs.

☐ Edit allows you to change the macro.

☐ Create lets you write a new macro (available when you enter a new Macro Name.)

☐ Delete permanently deletes the macro.

☐ Options lets you change the shortcut key and description.

There are several ways to run the macro:

● Select Macros from the Tools | Macro menu, click on the macro name and click on Run.

● If the macro was given a shortcut key, use that without selecting any menu option.

● Add the macro to a toolbar or menu and run it from there (see page 142).

You can also add a button to the worksheet and attach a macro to it (see page 143).

## Take note

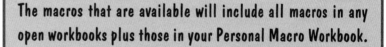

The macros that are available will include all macros in any open workbooks plus those in your Personal Macro Workbook.

Existing
macros

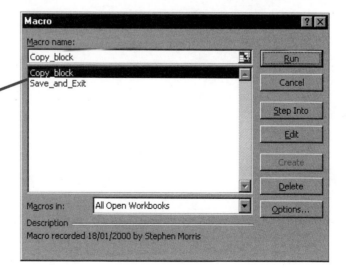

# Editing a macro

Macros are written and edited in the Visual Basic programming language. When you record a macro, Excel creates a Visual Basic procedure containing the necessary code. This code can be edited and new lines can be added. The Visual Basic code is stored in a separate area of the workbook, by default named **Module1**.

To edit a macro, Select Tools │ Macro │ Macros, click on the macro name and then on Edit.

Full details of Visual Basic procedures are given in the on-line Help. (If Visual Basic on-line Help was not included in the installation process, it can be added by re-running the Setup program.) Run the Excel Help program, click on the Contents tab and open the 'Programming Information' book.

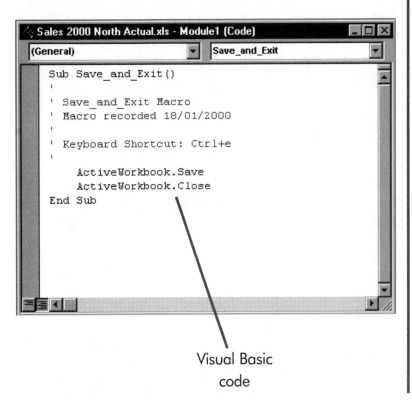

Visual Basic
code

To add a macro to a toolbar or menu:

1 Select Tools │ Customize.

2 Click on the Commands tab and the Macros category.

3 Drag the Custom Button to a toolbar or the Custom Menu Item to the menu bar.

4 Click on the Modify Selection button in the Customize box and then on Assign Macro. Click on a macro and then on OK.

5 Click on Modify Selection again. For a custom button, use Change Button Image to choose a new bitmap. For a menu item, type a new title in the Name box (include & in front of the shortcut letter).

6 Click on Close.

Clicking on the new toolbar button or menu item will now activate the macro.

142

# Adding buttons

To add a button to the worksheet:

1 Display the Forms toolbar by selecting View | Toolbars and clicking on Forms.

2 Click on the button icon.

3 Mark out the position for the button.

4 Assign a macro to the button by selecting from the macro list. Click on OK.

5 Edit the button name (click on the button text and then replace it with a more suitable name).

Although macros speed up frequently-used operations, the use of the Tools menu is not particularly convenient. Adding a command button to the sheet is a very simple process. A macro is attached to the button and then, to run the macro, all you have to do is click on the button. This is a particularly useful approach when setting up macros for other people to use.

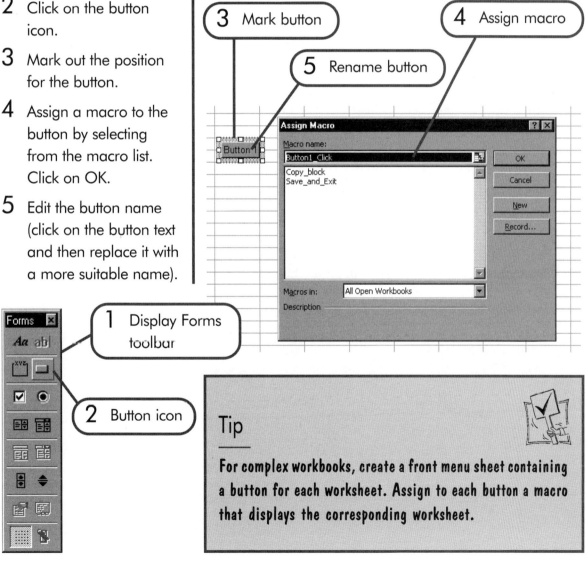

3 Mark button

4 Assign macro

5 Rename button

**Assign Macro**

Macro name:
Button1_Click

Copy_block
Save_and_Exit

OK

Cancel

New

Record...

Macros in: All Open Workbooks

Description

1 Display Forms toolbar

2 Button icon

Forms

## Tip

For complex workbooks, create a front menu sheet containing a button for each worksheet. Assign to each button a macro that displays the corresponding worksheet.

# Summary

❑ Data can be sorted into either ascending or descending order; the sort may be based on one or more columns and can be made case-sensitive.

❑ The Find and Replace options allow you to search for text or replace one text string with another throughout the worksheet.

❑ The toolbars can be customised and new toolbars can be created with any selection of buttons.

❑ Comments can be added to any cell with Insert|Comment.

❑ Bitmaps and other graphics can be overlaid on a worksheet using Insert | Picture.

❑ Macros are used to replay frequently-used command sequences or to provide more complex control over worksheet activities.

❑ Macros are written in the Visual Basic programming language and are stored in a separate module.

❑ Command buttons can be added to worksheets, with a macro associated with each button.

**144**

# 15 Record management

# Working with lists

A database contains data that is made up of **records**. Each record has the same structure, with its data held in a series of **fields**. For example, a database containing employee information would have fields for surname, forenames, employee number etc.; there would be one record for each employee.

Database programs such as Microsoft Access allow you to enter record-style data and are particularly useful where there are several different types of related record: for instance, employees' payroll and personnel records. However, Excel provides a good alternative for the entry of simple database records and gives you some effective methods for analysing such data.

In Excel, record-style data is entered in a **list**. Each row in the list represents one record, with each column containing the data for a particular field. An example of a worksheet for entering a list is given below. Each row contains a single transaction record. There are fields (columns) for the transaction number, date, company and so on.

To create a list:

1 Enter the field labels in a row on the worksheet, with no blank columns between them.

2 Format the field labels as text and apply a different typestyle to that of the main list (e.g. bold or a different point size).

3 On the second row, enter any formulae that are required.

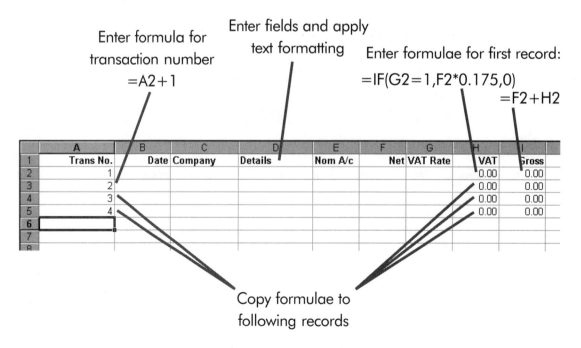

Enter formula for transaction number
=A2+1

Enter fields and apply text formatting

Enter formulae for first record:
=IF(G2=1,F2*0.175,0)
=F2+H2

Copy formulae to following records

|  | A | B | C | D | E | F | G | H | I |
|---|---|---|---|---|---|---|---|---|---|
| 1 | Trans No. | Date | Company | Details | Nom A/c | Net | VAT Rate | VAT | Gross |
| 2 | 1 |  |  |  |  |  |  | 0.00 | 0.00 |
| 3 | 2 |  |  |  |  |  |  | 0.00 | 0.00 |
| 4 | 3 |  |  |  |  |  |  | 0.00 | 0.00 |
| 5 | 4 |  |  |  |  |  |  | 0.00 | 0.00 |
| 6 |  |  |  |  |  |  |  |  |  |
| 7 |  |  |  |  |  |  |  |  |  |
| 8 |  |  |  |  |  |  |  |  |  |

**4** Copy the formulae to the next three rows.

**5** Enter the records by filling in the cells in each row. After the fourth record, any formulae will be copied down to the next row.

There are a few rules to follow when creating a list:

● Make sure that the format for the first row (containing field labels) is different in some way to that for the rest of the list, so that Excel can recognise the fields.

● Put each list on a different worksheet.

● If there is other data on the worksheet, put it either above or below the list (not to the left or right) and have at least one blank row between the data and the list.

● Do not insert blank rows or columns within the body of the list. If required, use cell borders to separate the row containing field labels from the records themselves, not a blank line or row of special characters.

● Don't hide rows or columns.

When you have created your list you can use all the usual Excel features for analysing the data. You can also use the Excel sort options to rearrange the list (see page 134); remember to click on the 'Header row' option in the Sort box.

| | A | B | C | D | E | F | G | H | I |
|---|---|---|---|---|---|---|---|---|---|
| 1 | Trans No. | Date | Company | Details | Nom A/c | Net | VAT Rate | VAT | Gross |
| 2 | 1 | 07/04/99 | Southbury S | Stationery | Stat | 12.34 | 1 | 2.16 | 14.50 |
| 3 | 2 | 08/04/99 | North Garage | Petrol | Fuel | 37.91 | 1 | 6.63 | 44.54 |
| 4 | 3 | 10/04/99 | Highfield SS | Petrol | Fuel | 39.34 | 1 | 6.88 | 46.22 |
| 5 | 4 | 13/04/99 | North Garage | Petrol | Fuel | 18.83 | 1 | 3.30 | 22.13 |
| 6 | 5 | 13/04/99 | Cellnet | Mobile | Mobile | 34.90 | 1 | 6.11 | 41.01 |
| 7 | 6 | 14/04/99 | Post Office | Stamps | Post | 10.40 | 0 | 0.00 | 10.40 |
| 8 | 7 | 16/04/99 | BT | Phone 1 | Tel | 91.48 | 1 | 16.01 | 107.49 |
| 9 | 8 | 16/04/99 | BT | Phone 2 | Tel | 191.37 | 1 | 33.49 | 224.86 |
| 10 | 9 | 16/04/99 | Highfield SS | Petrol | Fuel | 14.31 | 1 | 2.50 | 16.81 |
| 11 | 10 | 19/04/99 | Southbury S | Toner | Stat | 96.40 | 1 | 16.87 | 113.27 |
| 12 | 11 | 19/04/99 | Thames Trains | Ticket - Oxford | Trav | 14.50 | 0 | 0.00 | 14.50 |
| 13 | 12 | 21/04/99 | Post Office | Stamps | Post | 1.88 | 0 | 0.00 | 1.88 |
| 14 | 13 | 21/04/99 | Highfield SS | Petrol | Fuel | 18.50 | 1 | 3.24 | 21.74 |
| 15 | 14 | 22/04/99 | Evans | Sundries | Sun | 2.34 | 0 | 0.00 | 2.34 |
| 16 | 15 | 23/04/99 | Thames Trains | Ticket - Oxford | Trav | 14.50 | 0 | 0.00 | 14.50 |
| 17 | 16 | 28/04/99 | Highfield SS | Petrol | Fuel | 28.52 | 1 | 4.99 | 33.51 |
| 18 | 17 | 07/05/99 | Southbury S | Envelopes | Stat | 4.22 | 1 | 0.74 | 4.96 |
| 19 | 18 | 07/05/99 | Evans | Sundries | Sun | 0.56 | 0 | 0.00 | 0.56 |
| 20 | 19 | 11/05/99 | Evans | Glue | Sun | 1.84 | 0 | 0.00 | 1.84 |
| 21 | 20 | 11/05/99 | Thames Trains | Ticket - Kent | Trav | 18.71 | 0 | 0.00 | 18.71 |
| 22 | 21 | 13/05/99 | Cellnet | Mobile | Mobile | 42.70 | 1 | 7.47 | 50.17 |
| 23 | 22 | 14/05/99 | Post Office | Parcel | Post | 5.40 | 0 | 0.00 | 5.40 |
| 24 | 23 | 15/05/99 | Southbury S | A4 paper | Stat | 28.54 | 1 | 4.99 | 33.53 |
| 25 | 24 | 15/05/99 | Highfield SS | Petrol | Fuel | 19.43 | 1 | 3.40 | 22.83 |

# Data forms

When you have established a list on a worksheet (by filling in the first few records), you can use a **data form** to add, edit and delete records. A data form is a dialog box, generated by Excel, that allows you to work on one record at a time.

Data forms are particularly useful when the list is wider than the screen, saving you from having to scroll from one side to the other each time you make an entry or change a record. They also provide a simple data-entry method when other people are working on the list.

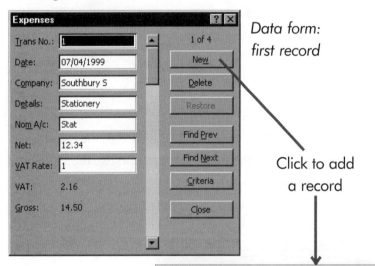

Data form:
first record

Click to add
a record

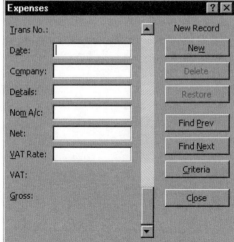

Data form:
new record

To display the data form for a list:

1 Click anywhere in the list.

2 Select Form (a hidden option) from the Data menu. The data form displays the first record.

To add a record:

1 Click on the New button.

2 Fill in the fields. Use [Tab] or [Shift] + [Tab] to move to the next or previous fields.

3 Press [Enter] to add the record to the list.

4 Add further records as required.

Take note

The Trans No field can be changed on the first record because the formula is applied from the second record onwards.

To edit a record:

1 Use the vertical scroll bar on the data form to locate the record.

2 Edit the field values.

3 Press [Enter] to save the changes. Any formulae will be recalculated.

To delete a record:

1 Use the vertical scroll bar on the data form to locate the record.

2 Click on the Delete button.

3 Confirm that the record is to be deleted.

Clicking on the New button displays a blank record, which you can fill in. The scroll bar on the data form allows you to locate a particular record, which you can edit or delete.

Current record
number

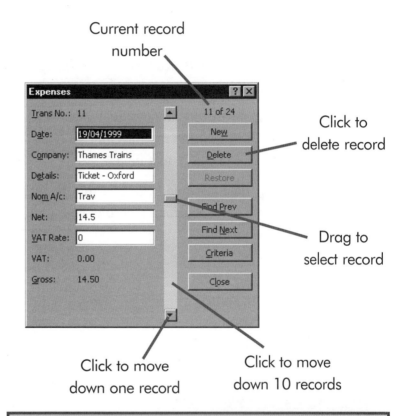

Click to
delete record

Drag to
select record

Click to move
down one record

Click to move
down 10 records

## Take note

If a field is calculated using a formula, you cannot enter the field on the data form. The field's value is calculated when the list is updated.

## Tip

You cannot use [Ctrl] + [Z] to undo changes made on the data form. Therefore you should always save the worksheet before opening the form.

If you don't want to keep the changes you have made, click on the Restore button before pressing [Enter].

# Finding records

The data form has buttons to help you find a particular record. The Criteria button displays a version of the form in which you can specify how you want to search:

- Enter a value in a numeric field to find records with exactly that value in the field.

- Enter one or more characters in a text field to find records where the value starts with those characters.

- Use >, <, >= and <= to compare the field value with the entered value (e.g. **>8** specifies that matching records must have a value greater than 8 in that field).

- Make an entry in more than one field to narrow the search. All criteria must be satisfied for a record to be found.

To search for a record:

1 Display the data form.

2 Click on the Criteria button.

3 Enter search criteria in one or more of the fields.

4 Click on Find Prev to go back to the previous matching record or Find Next to move on to the next match. The search always starts from the current record.

Enter one or more
values for comparison

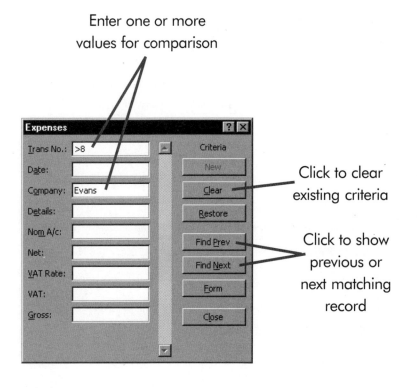

Click to clear
existing criteria

Click to show
previous or
next matching
record

Tip

If you want to display all the matching records as a list, use the AutoFilter and Advanced Filter options from the Data | Filter sub-menu (see opposite).

# Basic steps

# Filtering a list

To filter the list:

**1** Select Data | Filter | AutoFilter.

**2** Click on the drop-down arrow next to a field heading to select the filter criteria.

**3** Repeat for other columns if required.

The Advanced Filter feature allows you to devise even more complex filtering criteria.

Click to show filter options and select from drop-down list

Rather than step through a series of records that match specific criteria one at a time, you can temporarily hide all records that do not satisfy the criteria, leaving only those records that are of interest. This is achieved by **filtering** the list.

The AutoFilter feature allows you to select the filter criteria for one or more columns. The drop-down arrows next to the column labels change colour when criteria have been selected.

In each case, the following filter options are available:

- **(All)** cancels the filtering and displays all records.

- **(Top 10...)** displays the top or bottom records, depending on the values in the column. You can choose how many records to display (as an exact number or a percentage of the total number of records).

- **(Custom...)** lets you specify more complex criteria.

- The rest of the list contains all values that appear in the column so that you can choose a specific value.

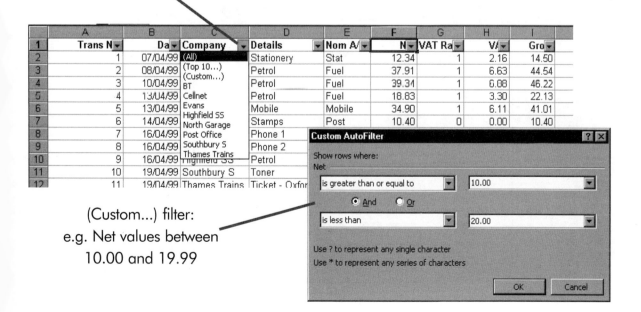

(Custom...) filter:
e.g. Net values between
10.00 and 19.99

# The Template Wizard

Data forms provide a simple way of entering records on a list but sometimes a more sophisticated approach is required. The Template Wizard allows you to set up a data-entry form on a worksheet template; the form is linked to a list on another workbook. The template is used for each new record, with a copy of the completed form saved as a separate worksheet each time; selected cells from the worksheet are then copied to the list.

This is a useful approach where only some of the data from the entry form is to be included in the list; it is also a good solution when the records on the list are to be created by a number of people. The first stage is to create the data-entry form; you can then activate the Template Wizard.

To create a data-entry template:

1 Start a new workbook and create your data-entry form. Include any formulae that are needed and format the form in any way you like.

2 Save the form as a normal Excel worksheet.

*Data-entry form*

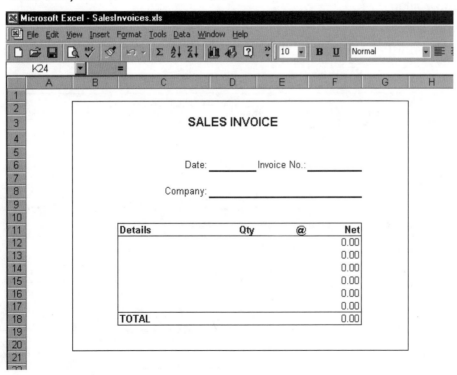

**3** Select Template Wizard from the Data menu.

**4** The workbook name and template name in Step 1 of the wizard should be all right, so click on Next.

**5** At Step 2, select the type of database you want to create. (Instead of an Excel list you can choose an Access or dBase database.)

**6** Select a folder and name for the database, then click on Next.

The Template Wizard consists of five steps, which guide you through the process of creating the template and database.

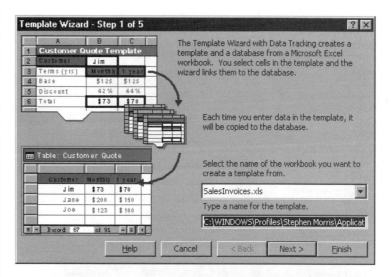

## Tip

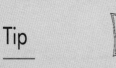

**The template must be held in your Templates folder (suggested as the default in Step 1). If the template is to be used by other people, it must be copied to their Template folders.**

## Take note

**The Template Wizard is an add-in program. If it is not included in the Data menu, it must be installed. Select Tools | Add-ins, tick the Template Wizard box and click on OK; then follow the instructions for installing the add-in.**

At Step 3 of the wizard you must specify all the fields you want to be copied to the database. In the next step, you can add in data from an existing workbook. The final step requires confirmation that you are ready to create the template.

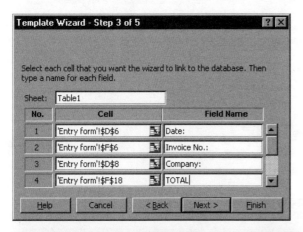

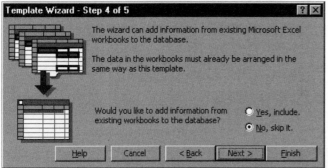

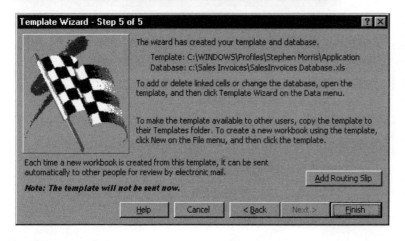

7 For each field to be included on the data-base, click on a 'Cell' box on the dialog box and then on the data cell you want from the worksheet. Then click on the corresponding 'Field Name' box; the field name will be taken from an adjacent label on the worksheet but can be changed if necessary. Click on Next when you have specified all the fields.

8 At Step 4, click on 'No' (unless you want the database to include data from an existing workbook). Click on Next.

9 At Step 5, check the details and then click on Finish. The template and database are created and are ready for you to enter data. Close the workbook from which the template was created.

# Using the template

To create a record:

**1** Select File | New and choose the template.

**2** Fill in the form.

**3** Select File | Save. Confirm that you want to create a record. Save the form with a unique name.

**4** You can inspect or edit the records by opening the database work-book.

New records are created by opening the template (don't click on the New button – use the File | New option), filling in the form and then saving it. The end result is an updated database and a separate workbook containing the contributory data.

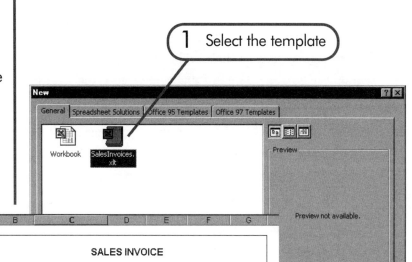

① Select the template

② Fill in the form

③ Save

④ View the database

## Tip

You can create templates for other purposes – just save any standard Excel workbook as a template (*.xlt) in your Templates folder.

# Summarising list data

When you have created a list, you need to be able to analyse the data and produce summary information. Excel provides a number of methods for doing this.

The simplest way of extracting totals is to use the COUNTIF and SUMIF functions.

- COUNTIF has as its arguments a search range and a criteria cell. It returns the number of occurrences in the search range of the value in the criteria cell (e.g. cell C3 below).

- SUMIF has arguments of a search range, a criteria cell and a data range. It returns the total of values in the data range for which the matching cell in the search range contains the value in the criteria cell (e.g. cell C4 below).

The example below uses the following formulae:

In C3:   =COUNTIF(C9:C58, C2)

In C4:   =SUMIF(C9:C58, C2, F9:F58)

In C5:   =IF(C3>0, C4/C3, 0)

You can summarise data in the following ways:

☐ To total the values in a block, use the SUM function or AutoSum button (see page 41).

☐ To get a temporary total of a block, mark the block and look at the sum shown in the status bar (hidden rows and columns are not included).

☐ To extract values based on the entries in a specific column, use the IF function (see page 46) or COUNTIF and SUMIF.

| | A | B | C | D | E | F | |
|---|---|---|---|---|---|---|---|
| 1 | | | | | | | |
| 2 | | Enter company: | Southbury S | | | | |
| 3 | **Number of transactions:** | | 4 | | | | |
| 4 | | **Total Net value:** | 141.50 | | | | |
| 5 | | **Average value:** | 35.38 | | | | |
| 6 | | | | | | | |
| 7 | | | | | | | |
| 8 | **Trans No.** | **Date** | **Company** | **Details** | **Nom A/c** | **Net** | **VAT** |
| 9 | 1 | 07/04/99 | Southbury S | Stationery | Stat | 12.34 | |
| 10 | 2 | 08/04/99 | North Garage | Petrol | Fuel | 37.91 | |
| 11 | 3 | 10/04/99 | Highfield SS | Petrol | Fuel | 39.34 | |
| 12 | 4 | 13/04/99 | North Garage | Petrol | Fuel | 18.83 | |
| 13 | 5 | 13/04/99 | Cellnet | Mobile | Mobile | 34.90 | |
| 14 | 6 | 14/04/99 | Post Office | Stamps | Post | 10.40 | |
| 15 | 7 | 16/04/99 | BT | Phone 1 | Tel | 91.48 | |
| 16 | 8 | 16/04/99 | BT | Phone 2 | Tel | 191.37 | |

Count the number of times the company in C2 occurs in column C

For all rows where the company in C2 appears in column C, total the values in column F

**156**

- ☐ To generate subtotals for each category, use Data | Subtotals.

- ☐ To generate totals using complex criteria, use the Conditional Sum Wizard (see page 158).

- ☐ To perform other tasks based on criteria, use the database functions. (For more information, search the on-line Help for 'Database functions'.)

- ☐ To provide a flexible summary table, use PivotTables (see page 162).

The automatic subtotalling feature adds a subtotal for each category. The list must be sorted according to the column containing the subtotal category (remember to mark the whole list before choosing the Sort option – see page 135). The Data | Subtotals option then allows you to decide how the subtotals will be applied.

In the example, the list has been sorted on Company and then subtotalled for each company, with subtotals for three of the columns. (The Trans No. column was removed before sorting.)

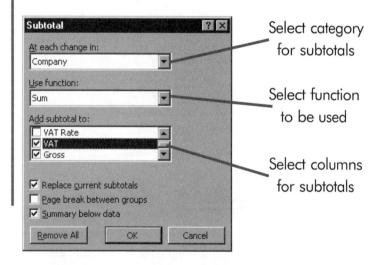

Select category for subtotals

Select function to be used

Select columns for subtotals

Click to hide detail; click again to expand

| 1 2 3 | | A | B | C | D | E | F | G | H |
|---|---|---|---|---|---|---|---|---|
| | 1 | Date | Company | Details | Nom A/c | Net | VAT Rate | VAT | Gross |
| | 2 | 16/04/99 | BT | Phone 1 | Tel | 91.48 | 1 | 16.01 | 107.49 |
| | 3 | 16/04/99 | BT | Phone 2 | Tel | 191.37 | 1 | 33.49 | 224.86 |
| | 4 | | BT Total | | | 282.85 | | 49.50 | 332.35 |
| | 5 | 13/04/99 | Cellnet | Mobile | Mobile | 34.90 | 1 | 6.11 | 41.01 |
| | 6 | 13/05/99 | Cellnet | Mobile | Mobile | 42.70 | 1 | 7.47 | 50.17 |
| | 7 | | Cellnet Total | | | 77.60 | | 13.58 | 91.18 |
| | 8 | 22/04/99 | Evans | Sundries | Sun | 2.34 | 0 | 0.00 | 2.34 |
| | 9 | 07/05/99 | Evans | Sundries | Sun | 0.56 | 0 | 0.00 | 0.56 |
| | 10 | 11/05/99 | Evans | Glue | Sun | 1.84 | 0 | 0.00 | 1.84 |
| | 11 | | Evans Total | | | 4.74 | | 0.00 | 4.74 |
| | 12 | 10/04/99 | Highfield SS | Petrol | Fuel | 39.34 | 1 | 6.88 | 46.22 |

# Conditional Sum Wizard

The SUMIF function allows you to add together all values in a particular category and the subtotal feature lets you do this for all categories in the table. For more complex tasks, however, you will need to use the Conditional Sum Wizard. This wizard generates a subtotal for a column based on one or more criteria: for example, whether a column contains a particular entry or is within a range of values.

1 Identify the list; the wizard should have found the correct range.

2 Specify the column for which you wish to produce a sum. Construct the criteria under which you want a record to be included. Click on Add Condition for each condition.

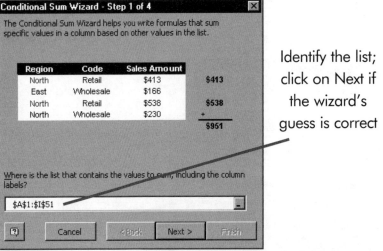

Identify the list; click on Next if the wizard's guess is correct

Select column to be totalled

Enter criterion in three parts

Click to add criterion to list

To remove a criterion, click on it and then on Remove Condition

158

3 Choose between displaying just the total or all the values used in the selection criteria.

4 Identify the location for the result. If you chose to display all values, this step will be repeated for each value.

The wizard places a complex condition in the cell you specify. You can add further conditions either by using the wizard again or by copying the formula and editing it.

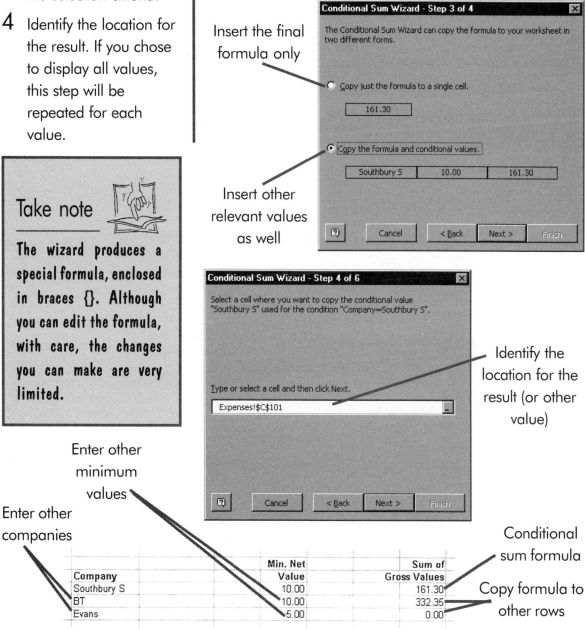

Insert the final formula only

Insert other relevant values as well

Identify the location for the result (or other value)

Enter other minimum values

Enter other companies

Conditional sum formula

Copy formula to other rows

| Company | Min. Net Value | Sum of Gross Values |
|---|---|---|
| Southbury S | 10.00 | 161.30 |
| BT | 10.00 | 332.35 |
| Evans | 5.00 | 0.00 |

# Summary

- An Excel **list** contains one record per row and one field per column.

- The first row in the list must contain the field headings and must be formatted differently to the rest of the list.

- Records can be added, edited or deleted using a data form.

- You can find records that satisfy simple criteria using the data form's Criteria button.

- A list can be **filtered**, so that it shows only those records that satisfy your criteria.

- The Template Wizard helps you to set up a data-entry form for filling a list.

- Each time you use the template, you create a worksheet containing the original data and the list is updated with the new record.

- The COUNTIF and SUMIF functions provide ways of summarising list data.

- You can insert subtotals in a sorted list.

- The Conditional Sum Wizard generates a subtotal based on a set of criteria.

# 16 PivotTables

# Using PivotTables

The task of setting up a worksheet can be time-consuming and difficult, particularly if there are complex formulae involved. However, once you have completed that part of the process, the task of presenting your results in a meaningful way can be filled with problems. If you want to summarise the results in a table, you have to make decisions about the detail you want to show and the way the table is to be laid out. When you have created the table, changing it to show a different viewpoint can take a great deal of time.

Similarly, if the raw data for your worksheet consists of a long list of items, in no particular order, constructing a summary worksheet can require a large number of formulae, containing complex If statements.

Excel's PivotTable feature helps overcome these problems by allowing you to generate a summary table from a block of data very quickly. You then have the ability to move the elements of the table around, giving you different views of the data in seconds.

## Example

The example below contains a list of expense transactions. A PivotTable will be used to summarise this information, including the total value for each company, nominal account and VAT rate.

Take note

**You can generate a PivotTable for any Excel list, providing it follows the rules described on pages 146–147.**

| | A | B | C | D | E | F | G | H | I |
|---|---|---|---|---|---|---|---|---|---|
| 1 | Trans No. | Date | Company | Details | Nom A/c | Net | VAT Rate | VAT | Gross |
| 2 | 1 | 07/04/99 | Southbury S | Stationery | Stat | 12.34 | 1 | 2.16 | 14.50 |
| 3 | 2 | 08/04/99 | North Garage | Petrol | Fuel | 37.91 | 1 | 6.63 | 44.54 |
| 4 | 3 | 10/04/99 | Highfield SS | Petrol | Fuel | 39.34 | 1 | 6.88 | 46.22 |
| 5 | 4 | 13/04/99 | North Garage | Petrol | Fuel | 18.83 | 1 | 3.30 | 22.13 |
| 6 | 5 | 13/04/99 | Cellnet | Mobile | Mobile | 34.90 | 1 | 6.11 | 41.01 |
| 7 | 6 | 14/04/99 | Post Office | Stamps | Post | 10.40 | 0 | 0.00 | 10.40 |
| 8 | 7 | 16/04/99 | BT | Phone 1 | Tel | 91.48 | 1 | 16.01 | 107.49 |
| 9 | 8 | 16/04/99 | BT | Phone 2 | Tel | 191.37 | 1 | 33.49 | 224.86 |
| 10 | 9 | 16/04/99 | Highfield SS | Petrol | Fuel | 14.31 | 1 | 2.50 | 16.81 |
| 11 | 10 | 19/04/99 | Southbury S | Toner | Stat | 96.40 | 1 | 16.87 | 113.27 |
| 12 | 11 | 19/04/99 | Thames Trains | Ticket - Oxford | Trav | 14.50 | 0 | 0.00 | 14.50 |
| 13 | 12 | 21/04/99 | Post Office | Stamps | Post | 1.88 | 0 | 0.00 | 1.88 |
| 14 | 13 | 21/04/99 | Highfield SS | Petrol | Fuel | 18.50 | 1 | 3.24 | 21.74 |
| 15 | 14 | 22/04/99 | Evans | Sundries | Sun | 2.34 | 0 | 0.00 | 2.34 |
| 16 | 15 | 23/04/99 | Thames Trains | Ticket - Oxford | Trav | 14.50 | 0 | 0.00 | 14.50 |
| 17 | 16 | 28/04/99 | Highfield SS | Petrol | Fuel | 28.52 | 1 | 4.99 | 33.51 |
| 18 | 17 | 07/05/99 | Southbury S | Envelopes | Stat | 4.22 | 1 | 0.74 | 4.96 |
| 19 | 18 | 07/05/99 | Evans | Sundries | Sun | 0.56 | 0 | 0.00 | 0.56 |

# PivotTable Wizard

To create a PivotTable:

1 Select PivotTable and PivotChart Report from the Data menu.

2 In Step 1, select the type of data for the report (e.g. Microsoft Excel) and the type of report (a PivotTable – you can add a chart later). Click on Next.

3 In Step 2, identify the data for the table. The wizard makes an intelligent guess but you can change the range if necessary. Click on Next.

4 In Step 3, identify the location for the table: either a new worksheet or an existing sheet.

5 Specify the format of the table by clicking on the Layout and Options buttons (see pages 164–166).

6 Click on Finish to create the table.

PivotTables are created using the PivotTable and PivotChart Wizard. (PivotCharts are described on page 171.) This wizard has three steps that help you to build an initial PivotTable, which you can then modify.

*Step 1*

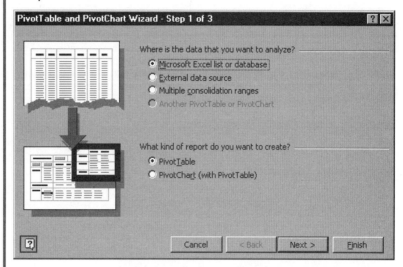

*Step 2*

*Step 3*

# Table layout

The PivotTable Wizard's Layout dialog box allows you to decide how the table will be laid out initially. The dialog box shows a representation of the table on the left and a set of buttons on the right. The buttons correspond to the data fields and are taken from the tops of the columns.

You specify the table layout by dragging the buttons onto the four sections of the table. For example, you may choose to analyse the Net amount spent for each VAT Rate, summarised by Company. The Net amount is the data; the Company and VAT Rate are the row and column headings.

If required, you can have more than one button in each section. For example, rows may be displayed for each Nominal Account within each Company (or vice versa).

Whatever your initial choices, they can easily be changed later.

## Basic steps

To specify the table layout:

**1** In Step 3 of the wizard, click the Layout button.

**2** For each field that you want to inspect, copy the corresponding button onto a table section. For example:

| | |
|---|---|
| **Row:** | **Company** |
| **Column:** | **VAT Rate** |
| **Data:** | **Net** |

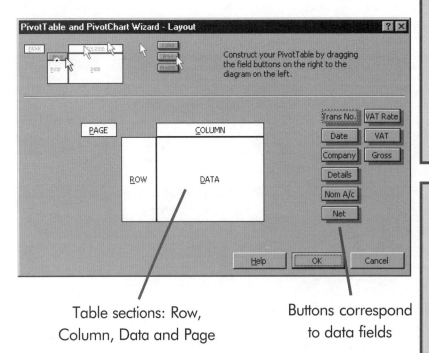

Table sections: Row, Column, Data and Page

Buttons correspond to data fields

## Take note

The Page section lets you select a value for one of the fields (e.g. display the table for one nominal account at a time).

## Tip

If you put a button in the wrong place, just drag it out of the table again.

**3** Double-click on the button in the Data field section (e.g. Count of Net). The PivotTable Field dialog box is displayed.

**4** Click on the type of summary you want (e.g. Sum instead of Count).

**5** If required, change the display format (Number button) and type of analysis (Options button).

**6** Click on OK to save the changes and then OK again on the Layout dialog box.

You have considerable control over the data that is displayed. The PivotTable combines all records for which the Row and Column entries are the same (for example, each entry in the Data section will represent all records for a particular Company and VAT Rate).

For each field dragged into the Data section, you can choose the way in which the data is summarised. Initially, the Wizard suggests that the table displays a count of the records but this can be changed to the sum of the values, their average and so on. You can also change the display format and the relationship of the values to some base value. For instance, you may show the Net value as a percentage of the Gross value. The 'Normal' option (the default) displays the actual value.

Double-click to change summarisation method

Click to change data type

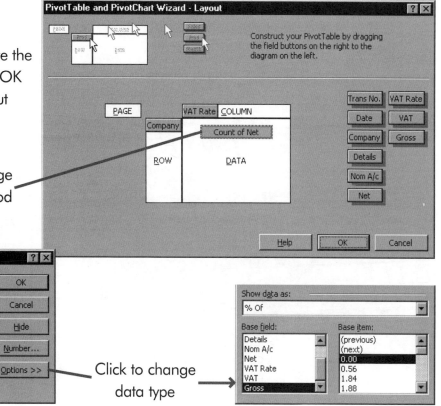

165

# Table options

The Options button on the final step of the PivotTable Wizard gives you the opportunity to change a number of features for your PivotTable. For example, you can choose whether grand totals are shown for each row and column, and the way in which errors and empty cells are handled. You can also specify whether the 'drilldown' facility is available, whereby you can expand the detail for a particular part of the table by double-clicking on a row or column label.

You can change the way the PivotTable is set up later (see page 168 for details).

Switch grand totals on or off

Choose display for errors and empty cells

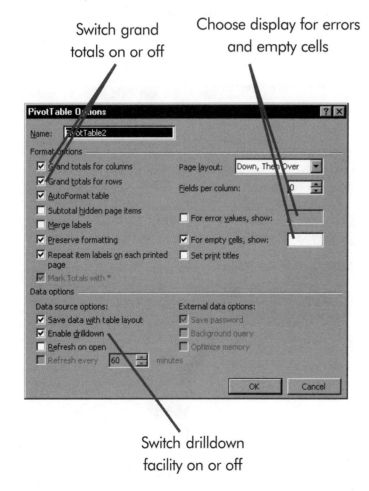

Switch drilldown facility on or off

## Basic steps

To change the PivotTable options:

1 In Step 3 of the PivotTable Wizard, click on the Options button.

2 Select the required options by clicking on the check boxes and making the appropriate entries in the text boxes.

3 Click on OK to accept the changed options and close the dialog box.

4 Click on Finish to complete the wizard and display the PivotTable.

Tip

The sample data used in this chapter can be downloaded from the Internet at http://www.madesimple.co.uk.

166

# Options

The table can be inspected as follows:

☐ Double-click on the Data label to change the type of data displayed (e.g. to change from Sum to Average).

☐ Click on the drop-down arrow on the Row and Column labels to list all possible entries; click on items to remove them from the table (click again to restore them).

☐ Double-click on an entry at the top of a column or on the left of a row to activate the 'drilldown' facility.

Change type of summary

Double-click a row heading to drill down to a further level of detail

# The PivotTable display

When you click on the Finish button on the PivotTable Wizard, the PivotTable is generated and displayed on its own worksheet (unless you have specified that it should be included on an existing worksheet). You can expand the level of detail shown or condense the table further.

If you double-click on a row or column heading you can 'drill down' to a further level. The fields are listed and when you choose one, the table will be expanded to show the detailed entries for the heading selected. Clicking on other headings shows or hides the same level of detail for those headings. Clicking on a heading on this second level allows you to drill down to a further level of detail.

Exclude/include specific items

Data and totals areas have been formatted with 2 decimal places

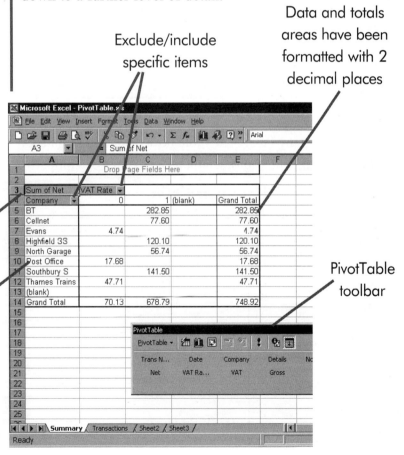

PivotTable toolbar

167

# Changing the table

You can change the way the table is displayed by dragging field labels in from the PivotTable toolbar. For example, if you drag the Nom A/c button onto the left of the table, the Company sections are expanded to show each nominal account.

| 3 | Sum of Net | | VAT Rate | | | |
|---|---|---|---|---|---|---|
| 4 | Company | Nom A/c | 0 | 1 | (blank) | Grand Total |
| 5 | BT | Tel | | 282.85 | | 282.85 |
| 6 | BT Total | | | 282.85 | | 282.85 |
| 7 | Cellnet | Mobile | | 77.60 | | 77.60 |
| 8 | Cellnet Total | | | 77.60 | | 77.60 |
| 9 | Evans | Sun | 4.74 | | | 4.74 |
| 10 | Evans Total | | 4.74 | | | 4.74 |
| 11 | Highfield SS | Fuel | | 120.10 | | 120.10 |
| 12 | Highfield SS Total | | | 120.10 | | 120.10 |
| 13 | North Garage | Fuel | | 56.74 | | 56.74 |
| 14 | North Garage Total | | | 56.74 | | 56.74 |
| 15 | Post Office | Post | 17.68 | | | 17.68 |
| 16 | Post Office Total | | 17.68 | | | 17.68 |
| 17 | Southbury S | Stat | | 141.50 | | 141.50 |
| 18 | Southbury S Total | | | 141.50 | | 141.50 |
| 19 | Thames Trains | Trav | 47.71 | | | 47.71 |
| 20 | Thames Trains Total | | 47.71 | | | 47.71 |
| 21 | (blank) | (blank) | | | | |
| 22 | (blank) Total | | | | | |
| 23 | Grand Total | | 70.13 | 678.79 | | 748.92 |

This is rather untidy, so you can drag the Nom A/c label to the left of the Company label. The table now displays the data by nominal account, with each account broken down by company.

| 3 | Sum of Net | | VAT Rate | | | |
|---|---|---|---|---|---|---|
| 4 | Nom A/c | Company | 0 | 1 | (blank) | Grand Total |
| 5 | Sun | Evans | 4.74 | | | 4.74 |
| 6 | Sun Total | | 4.74 | | | 4.74 |
| 7 | Fuel | Highfield SS | | 120.10 | | 120.10 |
| 8 | | North Garage | | 56.74 | | 56.74 |
| 9 | Fuel Total | | | 176.84 | | 176.84 |
| 10 | Mobile | Cellnet | | 77.60 | | 77.60 |
| 11 | Mobile Total | | | 77.60 | | 77.60 |
| 12 | Post | Post Office | 17.68 | | | 17.68 |
| 13 | Post Total | | 17.68 | | | 17.68 |
| 14 | Stat | Southbury S | | 141.50 | | 141.50 |
| 15 | Stat Total | | | 141.50 | | 141.50 |
| 16 | Tel | BT | | 282.85 | | 282.85 |
| 17 | Tel Total | | | 282.85 | | 282.85 |
| 18 | Trav | Thames Trains | 47.71 | | | 47.71 |
| 19 | Trav Total | | 47.71 | | | 47.71 |
| 20 | (blank) | (blank) | | | | |
| 21 | (blank) Total | | | | | |
| 22 | Grand Total | | 70.13 | 678.79 | | 748.92 |

## Tip

If you have created the table on a new worksheet, don't forget to rename the sheet straight away.

## Take note

If you click on the worksheet outside the table, the prompts and blue section dividers disappear; the PivotTable toolbar is also reduced in size. Clicking on the table again restores the prompts, lines and box. (The Hide Fields button on the PivotTable toolbar has the same effect.)

If you drag another field label into the data area, the table is shown with multiple columns. In this example, the table has been expanded to show the Sum of Gross values as well as Sum of Net, by dragging the Gross button onto the Data area and then the Data tab onto the Column area.

Table now shows a set of columns for each of the data sets (Net and Gross)

Click to list the data sets

| 3 | | | VAT Rate ▾ | Data ▾ | | | |
|---|---|---|---|---|---|---|---|
| 4 | | | 0 | | 1 | | (blank) |
| 5 | Nom A/c ▾ | Company ▾ | Sum of Net | Sum of Gross | Sum of Net | Sum of Gross | Sum of I |
| 6 | Sun | Evans | 4.74 | 4.74 | | | |
| 7 | Sun Total | | 4.74 | 4.74 | | | |
| 8 | Fuel | Highfield SS | | | 120.10 | 141.12 | |
| 9 | | North Garage | | | 56.74 | 66.67 | |
| 10 | Fuel Total | | | | 176.84 | 207.79 | |
| 11 | Mobile | Cellnet | | | 77.60 | 91.18 | |
| 12 | Mobile Total | | | | 77.60 | 91.18 | |
| 13 | Post | Post Office | 17.68 | 17.68 | | | |
| 14 | Post Total | | 17.68 | 17.68 | | | |
| 15 | Stat | Southbury S | | | 141.50 | 166.26 | |
| 16 | Stat Total | | | | 141.50 | 166.26 | |
| 17 | Tel | BT | | | 282.85 | 332.35 | |
| 18 | Tel Total | | | | 282.85 | 332.35 | |
| 19 | Trav | Thames Trains | 47.71 | 47.71 | | | |
| 20 | Trav Total | | 47.71 | 47.71 | | | |
| 21 | (blank) | (blank) | | | | | |
| 22 | (blank) Total | | | | | | |
| 23 | Grand Total | | 70.13 | 70.13 | 678.79 | 797.58 | |

To remove one of these sets of values, click on the arrow on the Data button and remove the tick from the appropriate check box.

Click to remove a data set

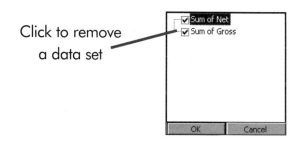

☑ Sum of Net
☑ Sum of Gross

OK    Cancel

You can tidy up the table by removing unwanted headings. For example, the '(blank)' heading for each field represents records where that field has been left blank; this can be removed if it is not used.

To inspect one section of the data at a time, drag a field label into the Page area. For example, if you drag Date into the Page area, the date is initially shown as '(All)' and there is no change to the table. However, if you now select a date from the drop-down Date box the table is updated to show data only for that date.

The usual formatting options are available: number formatting, colours and so on. However, if you change the PivotTable set-up you will have to re-apply the formatting.

You can change the way the report is displayed by right-clicking and selecting Format Report. There are ten formats to choose from, along with 'PivotTable Classic' (the original format) and '(None)'.

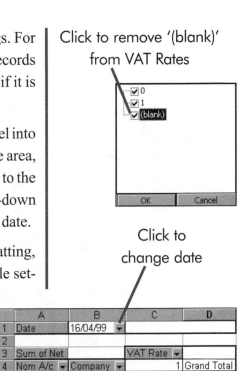

Click to remove '(blank)' from VAT Rates

Click to change date

| | A | B | C | D |
|---|---|---|---|---|
| 1 | Date | 16/04/99 | | |
| 2 | | | | |
| 3 | Sum of Net | | VAT Rate | |
| 4 | Nom A/c | Company | 1 | Grand Total |
| 5 | Fuel | Highfield SS | 14.31 | 14.31 |
| 6 | Fuel Total | | 14.31 | 14.31 |
| 7 | Tel | BT | 282.85 | 282.85 |
| 8 | Tel Total | | 282.85 | 282.85 |
| 9 | Grand Total | | 297.16 | 297.16 |

*Report 2*

| 3 | VAT Rate | Nom A/c | Company | Net |
|---|---|---|---|---|
| 4 | 0 | | | |
| 5 | | Sun | | |
| 6 | | | Evans | 4.74 |
| 7 | | Sun Total | | 4.74 |
| 8 | | Post | | |
| 9 | | | Post Office | 17.68 |
| 10 | | Post Total | | 17.68 |
| 11 | | Trav | | |
| 12 | | | Thames Trains | 47.71 |
| 13 | | Trav Total | | 47.71 |
| 14 | 0 Total | | | 70.13 |
| 15 | | | | |
| 16 | 1 | | | |
| 17 | | Fuel | | |
| 18 | | | Highfield SS | 120.10 |
| 19 | | | North Garage | 56.74 |
| 20 | | Fuel Total | | 176.84 |
| 21 | | Mobile | | |
| 22 | | | Cellnet | 77.60 |
| 23 | | Mobile Total | | 77.60 |
| 24 | | Stat | | |
| 25 | | | Southbury S | 141.50 |

*Format Report options*

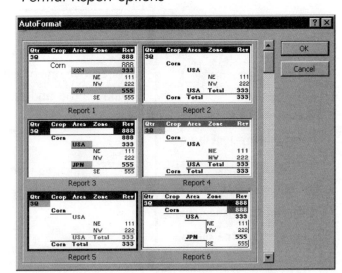

170

# Chart layout

# PivotCharts

The table and chart are related as follows:

☐ The Row headings become the X-axis labels.

☐ The Column headings become the data sets, shown in the legend.

☐ The Data values are translated into bars (or points on a graph).

☐ If there are multiple data sets, these are combined with the column headings in the legend.

☐ The Page setting determines which records are used.

## Take note

Generating a chart in this way has the same effect as if you had selected a PivotChart rather than a PivotTable at Step 1 of the wizard.

You can create a chart of the PivotTable (called a **PivotChart**) by clicking on the Chart Wizard button on the toolbar. Excel immediately generates a new chart sheet, which you can edit. The Chart toolbar works in the same way as for a normal chart, allowing you to amend the various elements of the display.

The sheet also has a PivotTable toolbar, which allows you to change the format of the table. For example, you can change the fields that are displayed by dragging field buttons onto or off the chart. Any changes you make to the chart are reflected in the PivotTable worksheet, and vice versa.

PivotTable toolbar

Chart toolbar

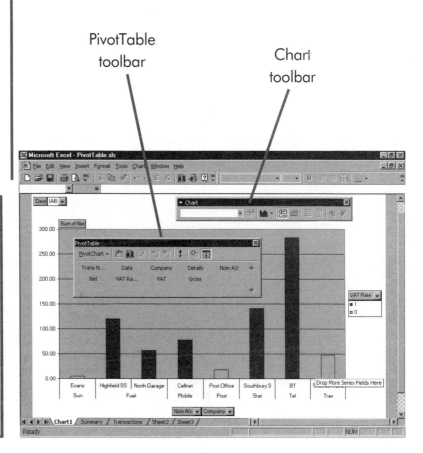

**171**

# Summary

❑ PivotTables show an interactive summary of a list; the summary can be changed by moving the row and column headings around.

❑ The PivotTable Wizard helps you to set up a PivotTable.

❑ The Layout dialog box lets you choose the initial layout for the table.

❑ The Options dialog box lets you change various features of the way the PivotTable works.

❑ Double-clicking on a row or column heading allows you to 'drill down' to a further level of detail.

❑ You can change the layout of the table by dragging field labels from the PivotTable toolbar or by dragging labels within the table.

❑ You can remove a field from the table by dragging it off the table.

❑ Unwanted categories can be removed for any of the fields.

❑ You can generate a PivotChart for any PivotTable. The chart has the same functionality as the table.

# 17 External databases

# Importing data

The previous two chapters considered how Excel can be used for storing and analysing database-style records. This chapter looks at ways in which such data can be imported from other sources and how Excel lists can be exported to database programs.

Excel can import several different types of record-based file, such as Access files, files from other spreadsheet and database programs, Word tables, comma-separated value (CSV) files and text files. Access files are considered on page 178. The other file formats are discussed here.

## Spreadsheet and database files

Excel contains converters that allow you to import files from several other spreadsheet and database programs, such as Lotus 1-2-3, QuattroPro and dBase. All you need to do to import these files is to open them as if they were standard Excel files. Spreadsheet files are imported with most of their formatting and formulae. Database files are imported as lists.

## Word tables

You can cut and paste data from tables in Word documents (or many other Windows applications). Mark the table in Word, press **[Ctrl]** + **[C]**, click on a blank cell in Excel and press **[Ctrl]** + **[V]**. The data will be copied, along with formatting features such as the font, borders and cell shading.

**Tip**

You can use the standard cut-and-paste options to transfer text or data from almost any other Windows program to an Excel cell. In most cases any formatting applied to the data will also be copied.

**Take note**

For information on file converters included with Excel, search the on-line Help for 'File format converters supplied with Microsoft Excel'.

*Word*

| Region | Volume | Amount | Notes |
|--------|--------|--------|-------|
| North  | 1204   | 2365   |       |
| East   | 879    | 1453   | Due to expand this month |
| South  | 2055   | 4503   |       |
| West   | 1773   | 3904   |       |

*Excel*

|   | A | B | C | D | E |
|---|---|---|---|---|---|
| 1 |   |   |   |   |   |
| 2 |   |   |   |   |   |
| 3 |   | Region | Volume | Amount | Notes |
| 4 |   | North | 1204 | 2365 |   |
|   |   | East | 879 | 1453 | Due to |
|   |   |   |   |   | expand |
| 5 |   |   |   |   | this month |
| 6 |   | South | 2055 | 4503 |   |
| 7 |   | West | 1773 | 3904 |   |
| 8 |   |   |   |   |   |
| 9 |   |   |   |   |   |

# Basic steps

To import a CSV file:

**1** Select File | Open and change the Type of File to Text Files.

**2** Choose the CSV file and click on Open.

**3** The file is imported as a list and can be reformatted. Save the worksheet as an XLS file.

## CSV files

Comma-separated value (CSV) files are text files in which each paragraph represents one record; individual fields within the record are separated by commas. Where the text for a single field contains a comma, the value is enclosed in quotes. (To avoid confusion, some CSV files enclose all text entries in quotes.)

Most applications can convert their data into CSV format. CSV files can be read into Excel, with one record per row and each field in a separate cell.

Field value enclosed in quotes when the data includes a comma

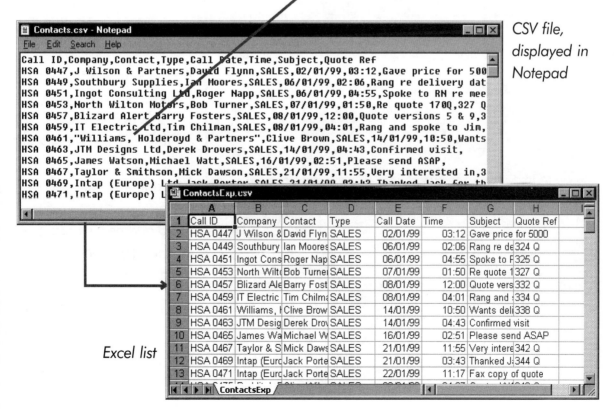

CSV file, displayed in Notepad

Excel list

# Importing text files

Most applications can create text files, with one record on each line. The files will either be delimited (where the fields on each line are separated by a tab or some other special character) or fixed width (where the values for each column line up, as on a printed report). Both types are imported into Excel using the Text Import Wizard.

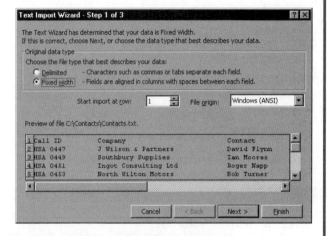

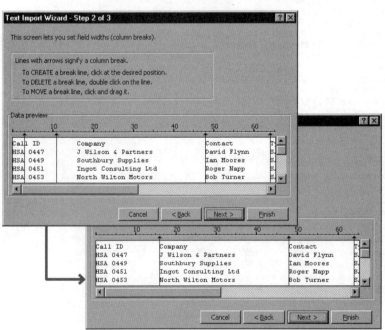

To import a text file, select File | Open, change the file type to 'Text files' and choose the required file. The File Import Wizard is activated. The wizard has three steps:

1 Choose the data type: Delimited or Fixed Width. The first row to import will usually be row 1 and will contain the column headings; change the row number if this is not the case. Click on Next.

2 Mark the start of each field with a vertical line. Excel suggests where these might be but you can drag them to new positions, double-click to delete them or click to add new vertical-line markers. Click on Next.

**3** Select the display type for each field. Click on Finish.

The data is imported in list format. You can then change the column widths and make other changes to the format, including the font applied to the field names in row 1. Save the file as an Excel (*.xls) file.

Excel suggests that each field has the General format. You can change this, where necessary. The formatting will be applied to all values in the column, apart from the field name.

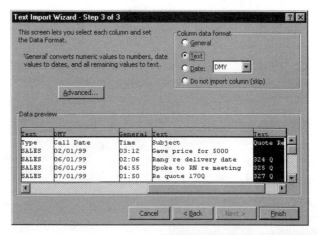

*Imported file*

| | A | B | C | D | E | F | G | H |
|---|---|---|---|---|---|---|---|---|
| 1 | Call ID | Company | Contact | Type | Call Date | Time | Subject | Quote Ref |
| 2 | HSA 0447 | J Wilson & | David Flyn | SALES | 02/01/99 | 03:12 | Gave price for 5000 | |
| 3 | HSA 0449 | Southbury | Ian Moores | SALES | 06/01/99 | 02:06 | Rang re de | 324 Q |
| 4 | HSA 0451 | Ingot Cons | Roger Nap | SALES | 06/01/99 | 04:55 | Spoke to F | 325 Q |
| 5 | HSA 0453 | North Wilt | Bob Turne | SALES | 07/01/99 | 01:50 | Re quote 1 | 327 Q |
| 6 | HSA 0457 | Blizard Ale | Barry Fost | SALES | 08/01/99 | 12:00 | Quote vers | 332 Q |
| 7 | HSA 0459 | IT Electric | Tim Chilma | SALES | 08/01/99 | 04:01 | Rang and | 334 Q |
| 8 | HSA 0461 | Williams, | Clive Brow | SALES | 14/01/99 | 10:50 | Wants deli | 338 Q |
| 9 | HSA 0463 | JTM Desig | Derek Drov | SALES | 14/01/99 | 04:43 | Confirmed visit | |
| 10 | HSA 0465 | James Wa | Michael W | SALES | 16/01/99 | 02:51 | Please send ASAP | |
| 11 | HSA 0467 | Taylor & S | Mick Daws | SALES | 21/01/99 | 11:55 | Very intere | 342 Q |
| 12 | HSA 0469 | Intap (Eurc | Jack Porte | SALES | 21/01/99 | 03:43 | Thanked J | 344 Q |
| 13 | HSA 0471 | Intap (Eurc | Jack Porte | SALES | 22/01/99 | 11:17 | Fax copy of quote | |

## Tip

**When importing times, leave the format as General; Excel converts the data into hh:mm format.**

*Reformatted worksheet*

| | A | B | C | D | E | F | G | H |
|---|---|---|---|---|---|---|---|---|
| 1 | Call ID | Company | Contact | Type | Call Date | Time | Subject | Quote |
| 2 | HSA 0447 | J Wilson & Partners | David Flynn | SALES | 02/01/99 | 03:12 | Gave price for 5000 | |
| 3 | HSA 0449 | Southbury Supplies | Ian Moores | SALES | 06/01/99 | 02:06 | Rang re delivery date | 324 Q |
| 4 | HSA 0451 | Ingot Consulting Ltd | Roger Napp | SALES | 06/01/99 | 04:55 | Spoke to RN re meeting | 325 Q |
| 5 | HSA 0453 | North Wilton Motors | Bob Turner | SALES | 07/01/99 | 01:50 | Re quote 170Q | 327 Q |
| 6 | HSA 0457 | Blizard Alert | Barry Fosters | SALES | 08/01/99 | 12:00 | Quote versions 5 & 9 | 332 Q |
| 7 | HSA 0459 | IT Electric Ltd | Tim Chilman | SALES | 08/01/99 | 04:01 | Rang and spoke to Jim | 334 Q |
| 8 | HSA 0461 | Williams, Holderoyd & Partners | Clive Brown | SALES | 14/01/99 | 10:50 | Wants delivery Monday | 338 Q |
| 9 | HSA 0463 | JTM Designs Ltd | Derek Drovers | SALES | 14/01/99 | 04:43 | Confirmed visit | |
| 10 | HSA 0465 | James Watson | Michael Watt | SALES | 16/01/99 | 02:51 | Please send ASAP | |
| 11 | HSA 0467 | Taylor & Smithson | Mick Dawson | SALES | 21/01/99 | 11:55 | Very interested in | 342 Q |
| 12 | HSA 0469 | Intap (Europe) Ltd | Jack Porter | SALES | 21/01/99 | 03:43 | Thanked Jack for the | 344 Q |
| 13 | HSA 0471 | Intap (Europe) Ltd | Jack Porter | SALES | 22/01/99 | 11:17 | Fax copy of quote | |

# Importing Access data

You can import data from Access into Excel in two ways:

- Copy a series of records (either whole records or just a selection of fields).

- Copy an entire table, form, report or the results of a query.

You can also use MS Query to import data based on a set of criteria and to merge data from different tables.

*Access table*

| Call ID | Company | Contact | Call Type | Call Date | Call Time | Subject | Quote ▲ |
|---|---|---|---|---|---|---|---|
| ▶ HSA 0447 | J Wilson & Part | David Flynn | SALES | 02/01/99 | 03:12 | Gave price for 5 | |
| HSA 0449 | Southbury Supp | Ian Moores | SALES | 06/01/99 | 02:06 | Rang re delivery | 324 Q |
| HSA 0451 | Ingot Consulting | Roger Napp | SALES | 06/01/99 | 04:55 | Spoke to RN re | 325 Q |
| HSA 0453 | North Wilton M | Bob Turner | SALES | 07/01/99 | 01:50 | Re quote 170Q | 327 Q |
| HSA 0457 | Blizard Alert | Barry Fosters | SALES | 08/01/99 | 12:00 | Quote versions | 332 Q |
| HSA 0459 | IT Electric Ltd | Tim Chilman | SALES | 08/01/99 | 04:01 | Rang and spoke | 334 Q |
| HSA 0461 | Williams, Holde | Clive Brown | SALES | 14/01/99 | 10:50 | Wants delivery | 338 Q |
| HSA 0463 | JTM Designs Lt | Derek Drovers | SALES | 14/01/99 | 04:43 | Confirmed visit | |
| HSA 0465 | James Watson | Michael Watt | SALES | 16/01/99 | 02:51 | Please send AS | |
| HSA 0467 | Taylor & Smiths | Mick Dawson | SALES | 21/01/99 | 11:55 | Very interested | 342 Q |
| HSA 0469 | Intap (Europe) L | Jack Porter | SALES | 21/01/99 | 03:43 | Thanked Jack f | 344 Q |
| HSA 0471 | Intap (Europe) L | Jack Porter | SALES | 22/01/99 | 11:17 | Fax copy of qu | |

Record: ◀◀ ◀ 2992 ▶ ▶◀ ▶▶ of 5555

*Excel worksheet*

| | A | B | C | D | E | F | G | H |
|---|---|---|---|---|---|---|---|---|
| 1 | Call ID | Company | Contact | Call Type | Call Date | Call Time | Subject | Quote Ref |
| 2 | HSA 0447 | J Wilson & Partners | David Flynn | SALES | 02/01/99 | ######## | Gave price for 5000 | |
| 3 | HSA 0449 | Southbury Supplies | Ian Moores | SALES | 06/01/99 | ######## | Rang re delivery date | 324 Q |
| 4 | HSA 0451 | Ingot Consulting Ltd | Roger Napp | SALES | 06/01/99 | ######## | Spoke to RN re meeting | 325 Q |
| 5 | HSA 0453 | North Wilton Motors | Bob Turner | SALES | 07/01/99 | ######## | Re quote 170Q | 327 Q |
| 6 | HSA 045 | | | | | | Quote | |
| 7 | HSA 045 | | | | | | | |
| 8 | HSA 046 | | | | | | | |

| | A | B | C | D | E | F | G | H |
|---|---|---|---|---|---|---|---|---|
| 1 | Call ID | Company | Contact | Call Type | Call Date | Call Time | Subject | Quote Ref |
| 2 | HSA 0447 | J Wilson & Partners | David Flynn | SALES | 02/01/99 | 3:12:00 AM | Gave price for 5000 | |
| 3 | HSA 0449 | Southbury Supplies | Ian Moores | SALES | 06/01/99 | 2:06:00 AM | Rang re delivery d | 324 Q |
| 4 | HSA 0451 | Ingot Consulting Ltd | Roger Napp | SALES | 06/01/99 | 4:55:00 AM | Spoke to RN re m | 325 Q |
| 5 | HSA 0453 | North Wilton Motors | Bob Turner | SALES | 07/01/99 | 1:50:00 AM | Re quote 170Q | 327 Q |
| 6 | HSA 0457 | Blizard Alert | Barry Fosters | SALES | 08/01/99 | 12:00:00 PM | Quote versions 5 & | 332 Q |
| 7 | HSA 0459 | IT Electric Ltd | Tim Chilman | SALES | 08/01/99 | 4:01:00 AM | Rang and spoke t | 334 Q |
| 8 | HSA 0461 | Williams, Holderoyd & Partners | Clive Brown | SALES | 14/01/99 | 10:50:00 AM | Wants delivery Mo | 338 Q |
| 9 | HSA 0463 | JTM Designs Ltd | Derek Drovers | SALES | 14/01/99 | 4:43:00 AM | Confirmed visit | |
| 10 | HSA 0465 | James Watson | Michael Watt | SALES | 16/01/99 | 2:51:00 AM | Please send ASAP | |
| 11 | HSA 0467 | Taylor & Smithson | Mick Dawson | SALES | 21/01/99 | 11:55:00 AM | Very interested in | 342 Q |
| 12 | HSA 0469 | Intap (Europe) Ltd | Jack Porter | SALES | 21/01/99 | 3:43:00 AM | Thanked Jack for t | 344 Q |
| 13 | HSA 0471 | Intap (Europe) Ltd | Jack Porter | SALES | 22/01/99 | 11:17:00 AM | Fax copy of quote | |

1 In Access, display the table you require and then mark a series of records or a block of data. (To mark a block, click on the top left-hand corner, hold down [Shift] and then click on the bottom-right corner.)

2 Press [Ctrl] + [C].

3 In Excel, click on the first cell where you want to paste the data.

4 Press [Ctrl] + [V]. The data is copied across with the relevant field headings.

5 Reformat the data.

# Basic steps

To copy a table, form, report or query:

1 In Access, open the table, form or report, or run the query.

2 Select Tools | Office Links | Analyze It With MS Excel. An Excel workbook is created and displayed.

3 In Excel, reformat the worksheet.

When you copy a complete table, form, report or the results of a query, Access creates a new Excel workbook with the name of the table etc. Excel is activated, if it is not already running, and you can reformat and edit the data in the usual way.

Click on A2 and select Window | Freeze Panes to show fields at top of sheet

Text columns have Wrap Text switched on, so only the end of the text is visible

*Excel workbook*

| | A | B | C | D | E | F | G | H |
|---|---|---|---|---|---|---|---|---|
| 1 | Call ID | Company | Contact | Call Type | Call Date | Call Time | Subject | Quote |
| 2993 | HSA 0447 | Partners | David Flynn | SALES | 02/01/99 | 3:12:00 AM | 5000 | |
| 2994 | HSA 0449 | Supplies | Ian Moores | SALES | 06/01/99 | 2:06:00 AM | date | 324 Q |
| 2995 | HSA 0451 | Consulting Ltd | Roger Napp | SALES | 06/01/99 | 4:55:00 AM | meeting | 325 Q |
| 2996 | HSA 0453 | Motors | Bob Turner | SALES | 07/01/99 | 1:50:00 AM | Re quote 170Q | 327 Q |
| 2997 | HSA 0457 | Blizard Alert | Barry Fosters | SALES | 08/01/99 | 12:00:00 PM | 5 & 9 | 332 Q |
| 2998 | HSA 0459 | IT Electric Ltd | Tim Chilman | SALES | 08/01/99 | 4:01:00 AM | spoke to Jim | 334 Q |
| 2999 | HSA 0461 | Holderoyd & | Clive Brown | SALES | 14/01/99 | 10:50:00 AM | Monday | 338 Q |
| 3000 | HSA 0463 | Ltd | Derek Drovers | SALES | 14/01/99 | 4:43:00 AM | Confirmed visit | |
| 3001 | HSA 0465 | James Watson | Michael Watt | SALES | 16/01/99 | 2:51:00 AM | ASAP | |
| 3002 | HSA 0467 | Smithson | Mick Dawson | SALES | 21/01/99 | 11:55:00 AM | in | 342 Q |
| 3003 | HSA 0469 | Ltd | Jack Porter | SALES | 21/01/99 | 3:43:00 AM | for the | 344 Q |
| 3004 | HSA 0471 | Ltd | Jack Porter | SALES | 22/01/99 | 11:17:00 AM | quote | |

## Take note

Any changes made in Access later will not be reflected in the Excel data. See page 186 for details of how to link Excel and Access.

## Tip

When importing a table, the text wraps over multiple lines; for a block, the AutoFit feature is also switched on. To change the display so that the left-hand edge of the text is visible on single-line rows, mark the text columns, select Format | Cells and clear the Wrap Text box on the Alignment tab.

# Exporting Excel data

You can export worksheets or data from Excel to other programs in a number of ways:

- Export a worksheet as a text or CSV file (which can be imported into many other applications).

- Copy a block of data to Word or PowerPoint (see page 190).

- Copy a block of data to Access (see page 182).

- Export a list from a worksheet to Access (see page 184).

The export of data as a text or CSV file is described here.

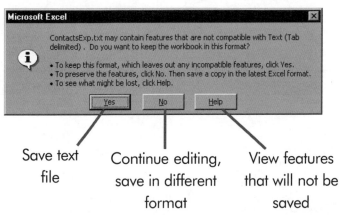

Save text file — Continue editing, save in different format — View features that will not be saved

*Tab delimited file*

To export a worksheet to a text file:

**1** Open the XLS file.

**2** Select File | Save As.

**3** Change the Save As Type entry to 'Text (Tab delimited) (*.txt)'.

**4** Excel changes the filename extension to TXT; change the main part of the filename if required.

**5** Click on Save.

**6** You are warned that some features may be lost (e.g. all formatting for text files). Click on Yes to continue. The file is saved and the new name is shown at the top of the Excel window.

**7** Close the workbook with File | Close.

**8** When you are asked if you want to save your changes, click on No (unless you have made changes since exporting the file).

The export of worksheets as CSV files is similar to that for text files. In this case, the Save As Type entry should be 'CSV (Comma delimited) (*.csv)'. Otherwise, the procedures are the same.

Excel creates a text file, with one record per paragraph and field values separated by commas. If a cell contains text that includes a comma, the text is enclosed in quotes.

*CSV file,*
*displayed in Notepad*

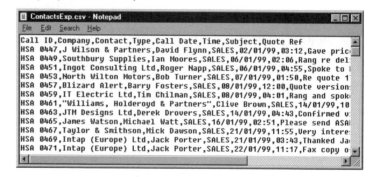

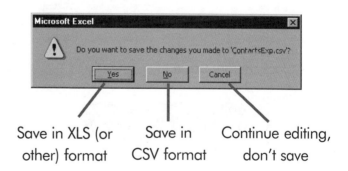

Save in XLS (or    Save in    Continue editing,
other) format    CSV format    don't save

# Exporting to Access

You can export data from Excel to Access in several ways:

- Copy a block of data to a number of existing records.

- Add a series of records to the end of a table.

- Copy an entire worksheet to a table.

Access validates the data as it is imported.

## Copying a block

You can copy a rectangular block from an Excel worksheet and overlay it on an Access table. However, you must make sure that the selected columns in the Excel worksheet match the corresponding columns in the Access table.

This is a useful procedure if you want to repair an Access file that has been damaged, where the data also exists in an Excel workbook.

*Excel block*

| North Wilton Motors | Bob Turner | SALES | 07/01/99 | 01:50 | R |
|---|---|---|---|---|---|
| Blizard Alert | Barry Fosters | SALES | 08/01/99 | 12:00 | Q |
| IT Electric Ltd | Tim Chilman | SALES | 08/01/99 | 04:01 | R |
| Williams, Holderoyd & Partners | Clive Brown | SALES | 14/01/99 | 10:50 | W |
| JTM Designs Ltd | Derek Drovers | SALES | 14/01/99 | 04:43 | C |

*Access block, before paste*

| North Wilton M | Bob Turner | SALES | | 07/01/99 | 01:50 | R |
|---|---|---|---|---|---|---|
| Blizard Alert | Barry ? | Support | | 08/01/91 | 12:00 | C |
| IT Electric Ltd | Tim Chilman | Support | | 08/01/91 | 04:01 | R |
| Williams, Holde | Clive B?? | Support | | 14/01/91 | 10:50 | V |
| JTM Designs Lt | Derek Drovers | SALES | | 14/01/99 | 04:43 | C |

*Access block, after paste*

| North Wilton M | Bob Turner | SALES | | 07/01/99 | 01:50 | R |
|---|---|---|---|---|---|---|
| Blizard Alert | Barry Fosters | SALES | | 08/01/99 | 12:00 | Q |
| IT Electric Ltd | Tim Chilman | SALES | | 08/01/99 | 04:01 | R |
| Williams, Holde | Clive Brown | SALES | | 14/01/99 | 10:50 | W |
| JTM Designs Lt | Derek Drovers | SALES | | 14/01/99 | 04:43 | C |

To copy a block of data to Access:

1 Mark a rectangular block in Excel. This can cover several records and need only include some of the fields. Press [Ctrl] + [C].

2 Mark a rectangular block in an Access table (using the [Shift] key). The block must be the same size and shape as the Excel block and must include the same fields. Press [Ctrl] + [V].

The Excel data replaces the existing Access data.

## Tip

**To mark an Access block, click on the cell in the top left corner, hold down [Shift] and then click on the cell in the bottom right corner.**

# Basic steps

To copy a series of records:

**1** Mark the rows in Excel. Press [Ctrl] + [C].

**2** Mark the blank row at the bottom of an Access table. The table must have fields that match the Excel data. Press [Ctrl] + [V].

The Excel data is added to the Access table.

# Adding records

You can copy complete rows of data from an Excel worksheet to an Access table. However, you must make sure that the data types in the Excel columns correspond exactly to the fields in the Access table.

This is useful where data is being created in an Excel worksheet but needs to be copied to a central Access database.

## Take note

**You will be asked for confirmation before the data is added to the table. If Access cannot add the data to the table for any reason (e.g. duplicate key values), the records are added to a new table called Paste Errors. You can inspect this table and then delete it.**

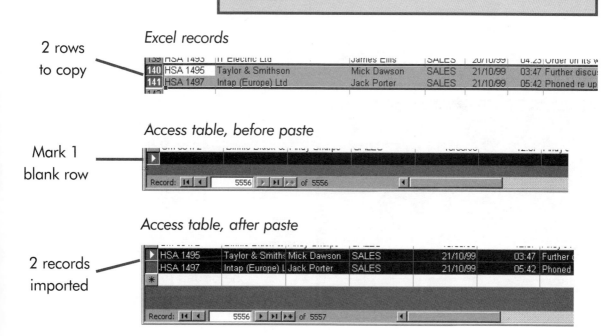

*Excel records*

2 rows to copy

*Access table, before paste*

Mark 1 blank row

*Access table, after paste*

2 records imported

## Copying a worksheet

You can import an entire Excel worksheet into Access. The worksheet either forms a new table or its records are added to an existing table. The import is controlled by the Import Spreadsheet Wizard.

To import a worksheet into Access:

1 Close the Excel work-book.

2 Open the Access data-base (or create a new database).

3 Select File | Get External Data | Import.

4 In the File Of Type box, select 'Microsoft Excel'.

5 Choose the Excel file and click on Import.

This starts the wizard, which has the following steps:

1 Specify whether or not the first row contains field names.

2 Decide whether you want the data to go in a new table or be added to an existing table. For an existing table, skip to Step 5.

*Step 1*

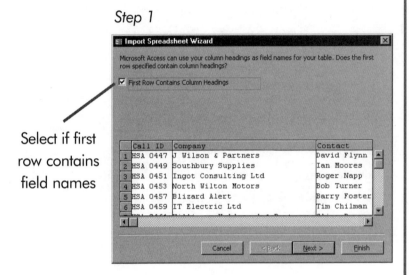

Select if first row contains field names

*Step 2*

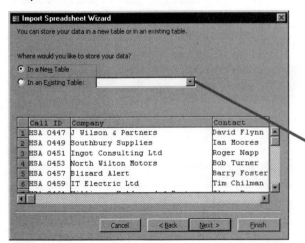

Select table if data is to be added to an existing table in the database

**3** For each column in the worksheet, specify the type of field you are creating.

**4** Identify the primary key field. (The entry in this field must be different for each record.)

**5** Enter the name of the new table.

The Import Spreadsheet Wizard guides you through the import process and helps you decide how the data is to be added to the database.

*Step 3*

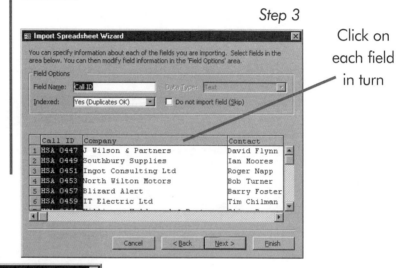

Click on each field in turn

*Step 4*

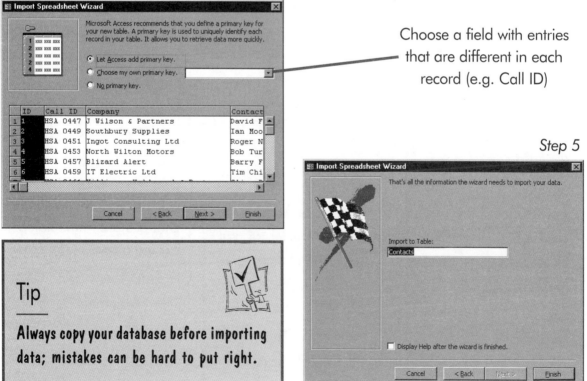

Choose a field with entries that are different in each record (e.g. Call ID)

*Step 5*

## Tip

**Always copy your database before importing data; mistakes can be hard to put right.**

# Linking to Access

As well as copying data between Excel and Access, you can create a permanent link between an Excel worksheet and an Access table, so that a change made in one is reflected in the other. The linking of the two files is controlled by the Link Spreadsheet Wizard.

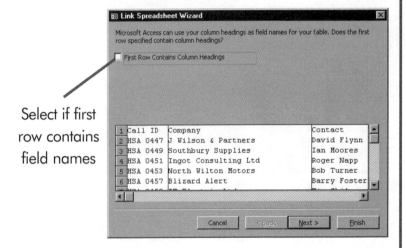

Select if first row contains field names

To link a worksheet to an Access table:

1 Open the Access database (or create a new database).

2 Select File | Get External Data | Link Tables.

3 In the File Of Type box, select 'Microsoft Excel'.

4 Choose the Excel file and click on Link.

This starts the wizard, which has just two steps:

1 Specify whether or not the first row contains field names.

2 Enter the name of the new table.

You can now make changes in either the worksheet or the table; the changes are immediately carried across to the other program.

## Take note

For the link to be successful both files must be open. Open the Excel workbook before the Access database, and close the workbook after closing the database.

## Tip

If you close the workbook before the database, you will get an endless series of errors in Access. The only way out is to press [Ctrl] + [Alt] + [Del] and end the Access task.

# Basic steps

To create an Access form for use with Excel:

1 In the Excel worksheet, select Data | MS Access Form. (This uses the Access Links add-in, which may have to be installed.)

2 Choose to create the form in either a new database or an existing database.

3 Use the Access Form Wizard to create the form.

When the form has been created it can be edited. The form is saved with the Access database.

*Completed Access form; can be edited*

If you want a more sophisticated entry form than that provided by the Excel data form, you can create an entry form in Access and use that for your Excel lists.

When you create the form, Excel adds a button to the worksheet. Clicking on this button activates the form. Entries made in the form are added to the Excel list.

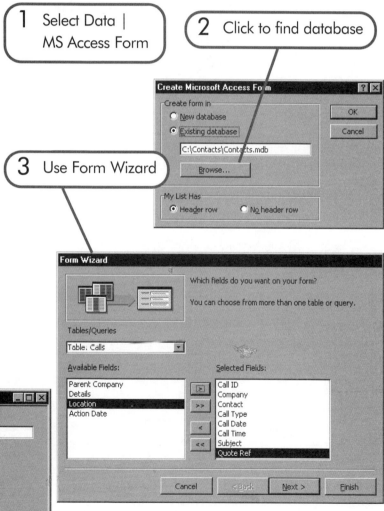

1 Select Data | MS Access Form

2 Click to find database

3 Use Form Wizard

# Summary

❑ You can import data from other spreadsheet and database programs, such as Lotus 1-2-3, QuattroPro and dBase.

❑ You can also cut and paste tables from Word documents.

❑ CSV files are text files with one record per paragraph and fields separated by commas. They can be imported into Excel by opening them using File | Open.

❑ Other text files are imported with the File Import Wizard.

❑ You can copy a block of data from an Access table using cut-and-paste commands.

❑ Access tables, forms, reports and queries can be exported to Excel.

❑ Excel data can be exported to text files, CSV files, Word documents, PowerPoint slides or Access databases.

❑ You can cut and paste a range of data from Excel to an Access table. You can also copy complete rows to Access.

❑ Excel worksheets can be imported into Access using the Import Spreadsheet Wizard.

❑ Excel worksheets can be linked to Access databases using the Link Spreadsheet Wizard.

# 18 Presentations

# Illustrating presentations

Excel data can be transferred in one form or another to most Windows applications. Apart from exporting data to another database or spreadsheet program (see page 180), Excel tables and charts can also be to illustrate Word documents, PowerPoint slides, Access reports and many other types of presentation. You can either copy a 'snapshot' of the data or create a link, so that the end product is updated whenever the Excel data changes.

Data can be copied with the Windows cut-and-paste features or using the Paste Special options.

## Cut and paste

The easiest way to copy data into another Windows application is to use the standard cut-and-paste features. The data is pasted in a format suitable for the application: e.g. a table in Word or a bitmap in Paint. PowerPoint displays an image of the Excel range; double-clicking on this lets you edit the data.

To copy and paste data:

1. In Excel, mark the range to be copied and press [Ctrl] + [C].

2. In the receiving application, click where you want to place the copy and press [Ctrl] + [V].

**Take note**

If a copied cell contains a formula, the result of the formula is copied, not the formula itself.

---

*Range marked in Excel PivotTable*

| Sum of Sales | | Qtr | | | | |
|---|---|---|---|---|---|---|
| Year | Area | Q1 | Q2 | Q3 | Q4 | Grand Total |
| 1999 | Central | 1185 | 954 | 1565 | 774 | 4478 |
| | North | 1048 | 625 | 1060 | 842 | 3595 |
| | South | 962 | 996 | 1398 | 850 | 4206 |
| | West | 1020 | 1084 | 1549 | 953 | 4606 |
| 1999 Total | | 4215 | 3659 | 5592 | 3419 | 16885 |
| 2000 | Central | 1263 | 1048 | 451 | 1263 | 4025 |

1 Mark range and select Edit | Copy

*Table in Word document*

| Sum of Sales | | Qtr | | | | |
|---|---|---|---|---|---|---|
| Year | Area | Q1 | Q2 | Q3 | Q4 | Grand T |
| 1999 | Central | 1185 | 954 | 1565 | 774 | 4478 |
| | North | 1048 | 625 | 1080 | 842 | 3595 |
| | South | 962 | 996 | 1398 | 850 | 4206 |
| | West | 1020 | 1084 | 1549 | 953 | 4606 |
| 1999 Total | | 4215 | 3659 | 5592 | 3419 | 16885 |

2 Click in application and select Edit | Paste

# Basic steps

To embed or link data:

1 In Excel, mark the range to be copied and press [Ctrl] + [C].

2 In the receiving application, click where you want to place the copy and select Edit | Paste Special.

3 Choose whether the data will be embedded (Paste) or linked (Paste Link).

4 In the 'As' box, select the format for the pasted data.

5 Click on OK.

Many Windows applications have a Paste Special option on the Edit menu. Using this option, data can be copied to the application in two ways:

● **Embedded data** is a copy of the Excel data or chart. Changes made in Excel are not reflected in the embedded data but you can edit the copy of the data.

● **Linked data** is not copied to the other application. Instead, the application loads the data directly from the original Excel file. Whenever the Excel data changes the linked data is updated immediately.

To embed or link data, the application must support Object Linking and Embedding (OLE); most applications do this.

When you choose the Paste Special option, you can decide whether the data is to be embedded or linked and you can select the format of the data.

Select format for pasted data; formats available depend on data type and receiving application

Embedded data

Linked data

Description of selected options

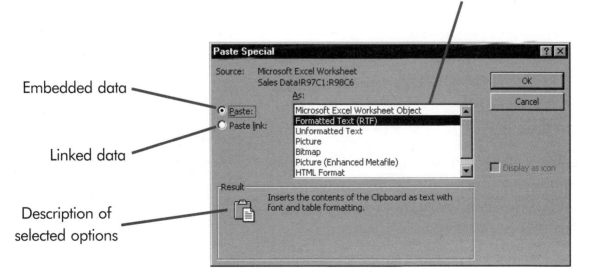

# Embedded data

When data is embedded in another application's file, the format you choose for the data determines the type of editing that is available. The examples below illustrate the range of options available when certain data formats are pasted into a Word document. The effects are similar for other applications.

## Unformatted Text

The data is pasted as simple text, with no formatting and the cell values separated by tabs. There is one paragraph for each worksheet row.

You can edit the text, change the font and apply all the usual formatting to each paragraph.

All formatting is lost

| Sum of Sales |  | Qtr |  |  |  |  |
|---|---|---|---|---|---|---|
| Year | Area | Q1 | Q2 | Q3 | Q4 | Grand Total |
| 1999 | Central | 1185 | 954 | 1565 | 774 | 4478 |
|  | North | 1048 | 625 | 1080 | 842 | 3595 |
|  | South | 962 | 996 | 1398 | 850 | 4206 |
|  | West | 1020 | 1084 | 1549 | 953 | 4606 |
| 1999 Total |  | 4215 | 3659 | 5592 | 3419 | 16885 |

Because tabs separate the data, columns will not line up until you change the default Word tab settings

## Formatted Text (RTF)

The data is pasted as a table, retaining all the fonts and cell formatting applied in the original. The result is very similar to that for simple cut-and-paste but the formatting applied to the table is slightly different.

You can edit the data or change any of the formatting features.

**Take note**

In PowerPoint, data pasted as Formatted Text is similar to that for Unformatted Text. Any font properties are carried across but cell formatting is lost.

**Tip**

PivotTables are pasted into other applications as if they were ordinary Excel ranges. The pasted table shows the data that was being displayed when it was copied to the Clipboard. You can only use the PivotTable functionality if the data is pasted as an Excel Worksheet Object.

# Microsoft Excel Worksheet Object

The range is pasted as an Excel table, keeping all character and cell formatting.

You can change the table size by dragging the sizing handles on the edges and corners. If you double-click on the table, an Excel worksheet window is overlaid, in which you can change the contents of the table. You can also scroll around the table, change the number of cells displayed or even select a different worksheet. When you click on another part of the document, the display is updated.

Table retains Excel formatting

Worksheet window overlaid for editing

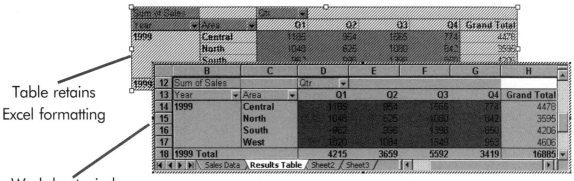

# Picture

The range is pasted as an image, using Picture format.

You can change the size of the picture by dragging the sizing handles, click on the picture to display the Picture toolbar or double-click to change the picture properties.

Picture toolbar

Drag to change picture size and shape

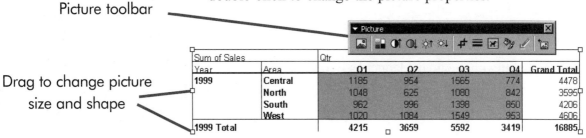

# Linked data

When you choose the Paste Special option and select the paste type as 'Paste Link', your document or presentation will show a representation of the data, taken directly from the original file. A link is created between the two files so that any changes made in the source data will be reflected in the pasted data.

The effects when certain data formats are pasted into a Word document are described here. The appearance of the data is similar to that for embedded data but the editing options are different.

## Unformatted Text

Although you can edit the pasted data, any changes you make will be overridden when the source data changes. However, you can make changes to the font for any part of the data and apply all the usual formatting.

## Formatted Text (RTF)

Any changes you make to the data or its formatting will be overridden when the Excel data changes.

## Microsoft Excel Worksheet Object

If you double-click on the table, Excel is launched and you can edit or reformat the source worksheet. The changes are carried across to the pasted version.

## Picture

Double-clicking on the image launches Excel and you can edit or reformat the original worksheet. The pasted image is updated with a new version.

**Take note**

When you paste a link into PowerPoint, the only formats available are the Excel Worksheet Object and a Hyperlink (which allows you to jump to the source data).

**Tip**

Always save both the Excel worksheet and the document or presentation before attempting to paste data (whether embedded or linked). The results may not be what you expect, particularly when you attempt to edit the embedded or linked data.

# Copying charts

Excel charts can be copied, embedded and linked to many other Windows applications. You can embed a chart in either Microsoft Excel Chart Object or Picture format. When linking a chart, only the Chart Object format is available.

If you paste or embed a chart, you can change its size or shape by dragging the sizing handles. When you double-click on the chart the Chart toolbar is displayed and you can change any feature of the display.

If you link to a chart, changes you make to the chart format will be overridden when the original data is edited. However, when you double-click on the chart, Excel is launched and you can revise the chart format there.

You can combine both data and charts in a single document or presentation, as illustrated below.

*PowerPoint slide*

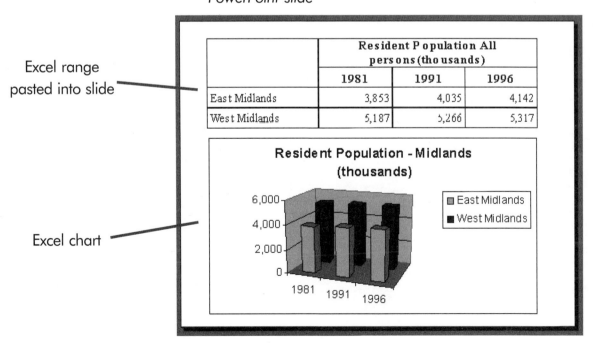

Excel range pasted into slide

Excel chart

# Summary

❑ A range of data from an Excel worksheet can be pasted into most other Windows applications, such as Word, PowerPoint and Paint.

❑ Object Linking and Embedding (OLE) lets you create a link between Excel and another application or paste data into the application.

❑ Embedded data can be pasted in a number of formats; the data can be edited but changes in the original worksheet are not copied across automatically.

❑ Data pasted as an Excel Worksheet Object can be edited in an Excel worksheet.

❑ When you create a link to a worksheet the data is not included in the document or presentation. If you attempt to edit the data you will be taken to the original Excel worksheet. Changes made in Excel are reflected in the copied version.

❑ You can embed an Excel chart in another application or create a link to a chart.

# 19 Internet access

# Hyperlinks

Excel worksheets can be linked in to the Internet in many different ways. You can add hyperlinks to Web pages, download data from the Internet to a worksheet or publish an Excel worksheet on the Web.

Hyperlinks provide a means of jumping directly to an Internet page. The link is displayed on the worksheet in the standard Internet style; by default, hyperlink text is blue and underlined. In the example, the worksheet shows a table of data copied from the Internet. The hyperlink below the table allows the user to jump to the Web page where the data originated.

To add a hyperlink:

1 Click on the cell where you want to place the hyperlink.

2 Select Insert | Hyperlink.

3 Click on the Web Page button to browse the Internet for the page you want.

4 Find the page. Return to Excel, where the 'Text To Display' and 'Web Page Name' will have been filled in.

Data copied
from the Internet

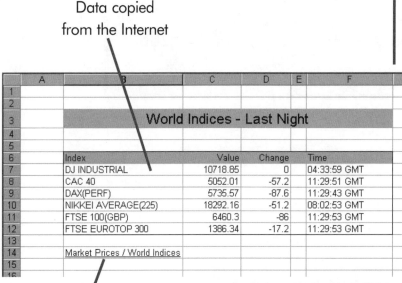

|   | A | B | C | D | E | F |
|---|---|---|---|---|---|---|
| 1 |   |   |   |   |   |   |
| 2 |   |   |   |   |   |   |
| 3 |   | World Indices - Last Night |   |   |   |   |
| 4 |   |   |   |   |   |   |
| 5 |   |   |   |   |   |   |
| 6 |   | Index | Value | Change | Time |   |
| 7 |   | DJ INDUSTRIAL | 10718.85 | 0 | 04:33:59 GMT |   |
| 8 |   | CAC 40 | 5052.01 | -57.2 | 11:29:51 GMT |   |
| 9 |   | DAX(PERF) | 5735.57 | -87.6 | 11:29:43 GMT |   |
| 10 |   | NIKKEI AVERAGE(225) | 18292.16 | -51.2 | 08:02:53 GMT |   |
| 11 |   | FTSE 100(GBP) | 6460.3 | -86 | 11:29:53 GMT |   |
| 12 |   | FTSE EUROTOP 300 | 1386.34 | -17.2 | 11:29:53 GMT |   |
| 13 |   |   |   |   |   |   |
| 14 |   | Market Prices / World Indices |   |   |   |   |
| 15 |   |   |   |   |   |   |
| 16 |   |   |   |   |   |   |

Hyperlink: click to
load Web page

## Tip

If you have to dial up to access the Internet, remember to disconnect as soon as you have found the page you want. Excel will make the connection for you but it will not disconnect.

**5** If necessary, change the text in the Text To Display box. This is the underlined phrase that will appear in the cell.

**6** Click on the ScreenTip button and enter the Help text you want to appear when the cursor is over the hyperlink.

**7** Click on OK to insert the hyperlink.

When the user clicks on the hyperlink, the Web page is located. If you do not have a permanent link to the Internet, the browser software is activated and the connection made.

Hyperlinks can be changed as follows:

● To edit a hyperlink, right-click on the link and select Hyperlink | Edit Hyperlink.

● To delete a hyperlink, right-click and select Hyperlink | Remove Hyperlink, then delete the link text.

● To highlight a hyperlink (e.g. to copy or move it), right-click and select Hyperlink | Select Hyperlink. Remember that you cannot select a hyperlink cell by clicking on it!

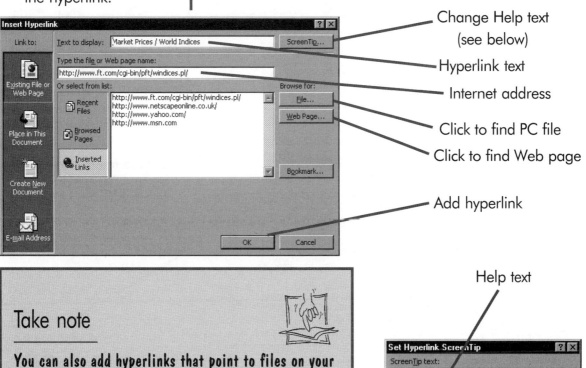

Change Help text (see below)

Hyperlink text

Internet address

Click to find PC file

Click to find Web page

Add hyperlink

Help text

## Take note

You can also add hyperlinks that point to files on your computer (e.g. Word files). When you click on the link the appropriate application is loaded.

# Copying Web data

You can copy data from the Internet using either Windows cut-and-paste or a Web query.

## Cut-and-paste

Attempting to cut and paste data directly from the Internet is not usually successful. The data tends to appear jumbled and requires considerable effort to make it presentable. However, you can usually copy Internet data by saving a Web page in HTML format and then cutting and pasting from that.

*Original Web site*

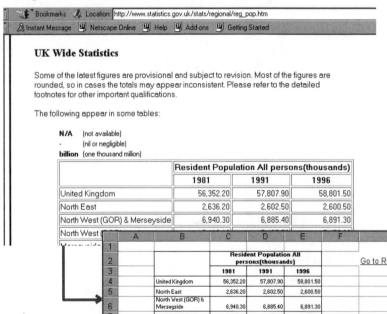

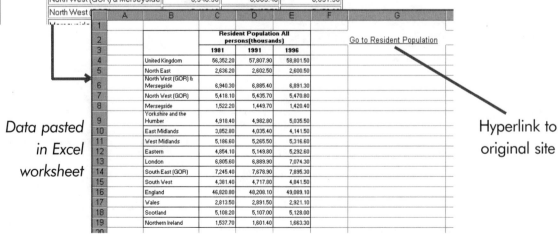

*Data pasted in Excel worksheet*

Hyperlink to original site

To cut and paste Web data:

1 Load the Web page you are interested in.

2 Save the page as an HTML file (browser's File | Save As option).

3 Working off-line, load the HTML file into a browser. Drag the pointer to higlight the table or text you want and press [Ctrl] + [C].

4 In Excel, click on a cell and press [Ctrl] + [V].

The copied data can be reformatted but if you want to get the latest version from the Internet you will have to repeat the process.

# Basic steps

To run a Web query:

**1** In Excel, click on the blank cell that will be the top left-hand corner of the Web data block.

**2** Select Data | Get External Data | New Web Query.

**3** If you know the Web address, enter it. Otherwise, click on the Browse Web button, select the page using your browser and return to Excel, where the address should have been pasted in.

**4** Click on the option buttons to choose the data you want (usually, Only The Tables) and the type of formatting (Full HTML Formatting).

## Web queries

A Web query inserts a block of data taken directly from a Web page. The block can be updated when the original data changes. This avoids the need for saving the page as an HTML file but there are limitations on how you can format the end result.

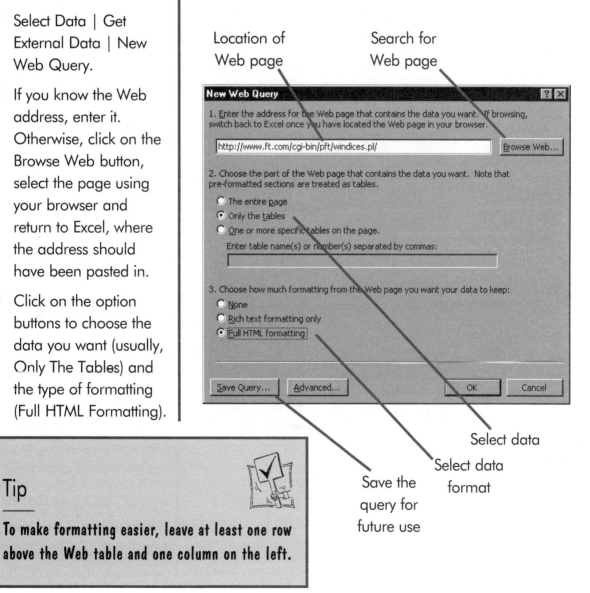

Location of Web page

Search for Web page

Select data

Select data format

Save the query for future use

## Tip

To make formatting easier, leave at least one row above the Web table and one column on the left.

The details of the Web query can be saved in a file, with an IQY extension. This allows you to re-run a query at any time or to load an existing query and amend it.

Select location for Web table

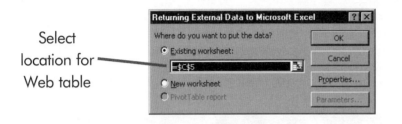

Decide when table will be refreshed

Formatting options

Decide what will happen when table size changes

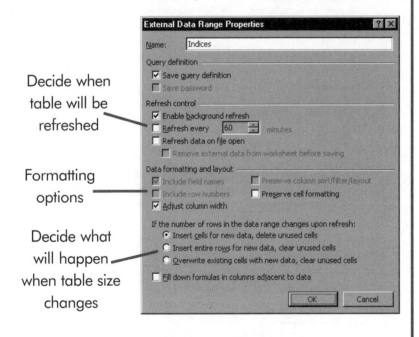

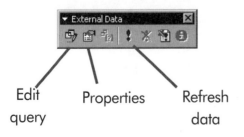

Edit query

Properties

Refresh data

5 Click on Save Query to save the query as an IQY file. Click on OK to close the New Web Query box.

6 In the Returning Excel Query dialog box, identify the location for the Web data (the default is the current cell).

7 Click on Properties to change the way in which the data is displayed and updated. Then click on OK.

8 Click on OK in the Returning Excel Query box.

There will be a pause while Excel retrieves the data. (A 'Getting Data' message is displayed.) The table of Web data will then be added to the worksheet and the External Data toolbar will be displayed.

You can re-run the query at any time with Data | Get External Data | Run Saved Query.

The Web data is often more than you really want, as some of the other data on the page may have been interpreted as tables. However, the changes you can make to the data are restricted if you want to be able to refresh the data when the Web page changes.

Essentially, the changes you can make are limited to hiding unwanted rows and columns. Any alterations to column height or width, or formatting of cells and text, will be overridden when the table is refreshed.

You can refresh a table at any time by clicking on the Refresh Data button on the External Data toolbar.

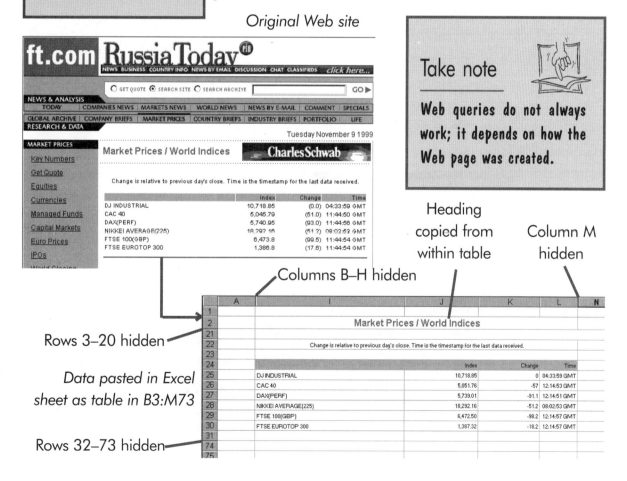

*Original Web site*

Heading copied from within table

Column M hidden

Columns B–H hidden

Rows 3–20 hidden

*Data pasted in Excel sheet as table in B3:M73*

Rows 32–73 hidden

# Publishing Excel data

You can save either a whole workbook or just part of a worksheet as a Web page. This can then be uploaded to your Web site and made available for others to see and use.

There are three ways of publishing your data:

● Non-interactive: users can view your data but cannot change it.

● Interactive, with spreadsheet functionality: users can view your data and apply standard Excel features (e.g. sorting, summing blocks).

● Interactive, with PivotTable functionality: users can apply the usual PivotTable operations to your data; the table can be refreshed when the original data changes.

Users can view non-interactive data with any browser; however, for interactive data, they must have the Office Web Components (which are installed as part of Office 2000) and be using Internet Explorer 4.01 or a later version. This will limit your audience.

To publish data on the Internet:

1 Select File | Save As.

2 Change the Save As Type to 'Web Page'.

3 Click on the Publish button.

4 Select the data you want to publish (e.g. the whole sheet or just a PivotTable).

5 Select the type of interactivity.

6 Click on the Change button and enter a title for the page.

7 Enter a filename (including the location of the Web page: either a folder on your hard disk or a Web server).

8 Click on the Publish button.

The file is saved as an HTML file. If you publish as a PivotTable, Excel creates a special folder to store related files.

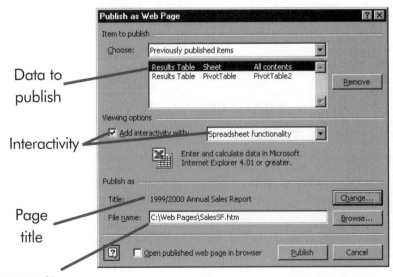

Data to publish

Interactivity

Page title

HTML filename

204

# Notes

□ You should save the XLS file before publishing, so that you can go back to the original if necessary.

□ You can preview the file using File | Web Page Preview (though the interactive features are not shown). Alternatively, load the HTML file into any Web browser.

□ You can update the HTML file with a new version by clicking on the Republish option on the Save As dialog box.

□ If you select an existing filename when publishing you can choose to add your data to the file; the data is added at the bottom of the file.

□ If you move or copy a PivotTable HTML file, you must also move or copy the associated 'Files' folder.

After publishing your data as an HTML file you can use any Web designer software (such as FronPage) to reformat the data and improve the appearance of the page.

*Excel worksheet*

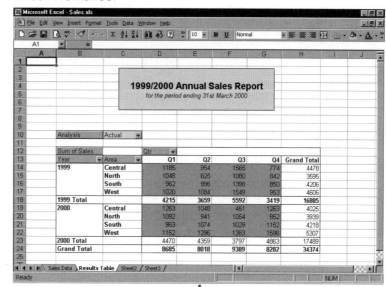

*Web page*                    *(Spreadsheet functionality)*

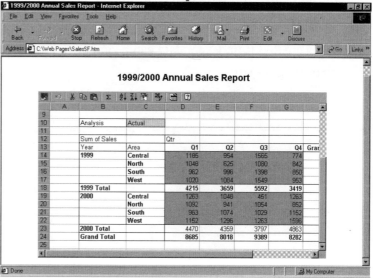

**205**

# Summary

- ❑ Hyperlinks to Internet pages can be added to Excel worksheets.

- ❑ When a user clicks on the hyperlink, the Web page is located and displayed.

- ❑ Cutting and pasting directly from Web pages is not usually successful.

- ❑ Web pages can be saved as HTML files and the data can then be copied into Excel.

- ❑ A Web query inserts a block of data from a Web page directly into an Excel sheet.

- ❑ Web queries can be saved as IQY files for later use.

- ❑ You can only make limited changes to Web data, particularly if you want to refresh it later.

- ❑ Excel data can be published to a Web page.

- ❑ Non-interactive data can be viewed by any Internet user.

- ❑ Interactive data can be manipulated by other users, providing they have the Office Web Components and Internet Explorer 4.01 or later.

- ❑ Pages created from Excel data can be enhanced using any Web designer software.

# Index

Typeface, 84

## U

Undo options, 17, 96
Unformatted text (export), 192, 194

## V

View | Toolbars, 137
Visual Basic, 142

## W

Web pages
    copying, 200
    hyperlinks, 198
Web queries, 201
    saving, 202
Width of columns, 72
Window size, 4
Window | Freeze Panes, 80
Window | New Window, 98
Windows
    changing, 23
    multiple, 98

Word tables
    exporting to, 190
    importing, 174
Workbooks, 94
    printing, 131
Worksheets, 6
    automating, 140
    closing, 24
    copying, 101
    deleting, 100
    grouping, 99
    inserting, 100
    loading, 25
    moving, 101
    moving around, 7
    multiple, 94
    new, 96
    printing, 131
    renaming, 22, 95
    saving, 20
    windows, 23

## X

XLS extension, 21
XLT extension, 155